PITMAN
SHORTHAND

NEW COURSE
KEY

Isaac Pitman

PITMAN

PITMAN PUBLISHING LIMITED
39 Parker Street, London WC2B 5PB

Associated Companies
Copp Clark Ltd, Toronto · Fearon-Pitman Publishers Inc, Belmont, California · Pitman Publishing Co. SA (Pty) Ltd, Johannesburg · Pitman Publishing New Zealand Ltd, Wellington · Pitman Publishing Pty Ltd, Melbourne

ISBN: 0 273 00957 5

Text set in 9/10 pt. Monotype Times New Roman, printed by letterpress, and bound in Great Britain at The Pitman Press, Bath
G7—(S.185:24)

Exercise 1

1. *The* date. 2. *The* page. 3. Date-*the* page. 4. *The* debt. 5. Pay-*the* debt. 6. *Who* paid-*the* debt? 7. Abe Page paid *it, but* Ted Day paid *it, too.* 8. Ted paid-*the* debt *which* Abe paid. 9. *The* day Abe paid-*the* debt, Ted paid *it, too.* 10. *Do* page *two.* 11. Aid Ed *to-do it* 12. Pay Ted *to* aid Abe.

Exercise 2

1. *Have*-they paid-*the* debt? 2. They-*think-the* debt *was* paid. 3. *Do* they say so? 4. They say they paid *it to* Abe. 5. They-*have usually* paid us. 6. *Was-it* paid *to* Joe? 7. *Shall* they show *the* essay *to* Joe? 8. *Who shall* judge-*the* essay? 9. Abe *shall-be-the* judge.

Exercise 3

1. Show *them-the* boat. 2. *Who shall* fetch-*the* boat? 3. *Which* boat *shall* Joe show *to-them*? 4. They-*have usually* paid us *to-do it, but* they-*have* paid Ed, *too.* 5. They both say so. 6. They-*think* they-*have to* vote *to* aid *them.* 7. *Which-was-the* page they showed us? 8. *Who-was* up *to* page *two*? 9. They both say *it-was usual to* vote.

Exercise 4

1. They-*will come to-the* game *to*day. 2. They-*think* they-will-*be* delayed. 3. Show *them-the* way *to-the* lake. 4. *Who*-will *come to-the* boat? 5. *Do* they-*think we-shall* beg *them to-come*? 6. *We*-may change-*the* date *to-the* tenth. 7. *Do* they know-*the* date?

Exercise 5

1. *Have-we* paid-*the* debt? 2. *We-have given him the* cheque *to* mail *to-them to*day. 3. *Shall we* take-*the* mail *to-the* boat? 4. *We-shall* aim *to* change-*the* name. 5. *We*-know they-will *come to*day. 6. They-will take-*the* lunch *to-the* lake. 7. Joe led-*the* way *to-the* lake, *but*-they say *it-was too*-low *to* bathe. 8. *Was-the* mail delayed? 9. *It*-will-*be* given *to him to*day.

Exercise 6

1. Joe owes *them-the* debt, so *we-have given them-the* cheque. 2. *The thing to-do was to*-make *them* weigh *the* coal. 3. They both say-*the* coal

3

was weighed. 4. *Who*-came *to*-take-*the* load *to-the* depot? 5. *We-have*-no lunch *to*-take *to-the* game. 6. May-*we-have-the* yellow boat *to*-take *to-the* bay? 7. *Who*-will-*be* paid *to* show *them-the* way *to-do* *it*? 8. *We-think* they-will *come to-the* show *which*-will-*be given to*day.

Exercise 7

1. *Who*-will *come to* fetch-*the* cash? *We-shall-be* at-*the* bank at *two*.
2. *We*-know-*the* debt *was* paid. *A* cheque *was given to him* long-ago.
3. *We* saw *them* at-*the* shop. They bought *a* ball *for* Jack.
4. They got *a* doll *for* Ann, *too*.
5. May-*we-have a* cheque *for-the* bag bought *on-the* tenth *of*-May?
6. *We*-know they-*had a* long talk, *but-we-think* they-will *give him* no cash.
7. They say Bob owes-*the* debt, *but-the* watch *was* paid *for on-the* tenth.
8. *We-think-the* chalk may damage-*the* bag. No, *it*-will *come* off. Wash *it* off.
9. Ask Paul *to* attach *a* tag *to-the* top *of-the* bag.
10. *We-shall* check-*the* damage *to-the* boat.

Exercise 8

1. *The* tall lad *was* paid 3s. 6d. *a* day *to*-watch-*the* shop.
2. *The* lake *was* calm, so *we* came back *on-the* boat.
3. *It-was an* odd *thing to-do*, but *it-was a* shame *to*-laugh at *him*.
4. *Which of-them* saw-*the* lad take-*the* package back *to-the* shop?
5. Paul may manage *to* show *them the* way *to-do-the* job.
6. *We*-know they-will-*be* at-*the* game, *but*-they-will *come* back *for-the* show.
7. *We-think* they take *too*-long *to-do-the* job. *We-have* usually given-*the* job *to-them*, *but-we*-may make *a* change.
8. They-will pay *for-the* damage *to-the* tank, *but-we-think* they-will ask *for a* delay.
9. *We-had* no cash *to* pay *him* at-*the* shop, so *a* cheque *was given to him*.
10. Pam *had to-come a* long way, *but* saw-*the* game.

Exercise 9

1. They-will-*be* at-*the* show *which*-will-*be given* on 29th-May. *It*-will-*be* on *a* Monday.

2. *We-shall* get enough cash at-*the* bank *to* pay both *of-them for-the* job.
3. *Usually we* engage *a* bungalow at-*the* lake *for a* month.
4. *The* wage they paid *was too* low, so Tom *had to-give* up-*the* job.
5. *We*-know-*the* debt *was* unpaid, *but*-they *had* no cash.
6. *Who*-will aid Anna *to*-get-*the* mail *for* Bath off at *two*?
7. *We-think* they-will take-*the* boat *for* Canada *on*-Monday, 12th-May.
8. *The* envelope *for-the* mail *was on* top *of-the* pad.
9. *We-shall-have to* ask *him to* pay *for-the* damage *to-the* gate.
10. *We* saw *them* at-*the* game, *which-was on*-Monday, *the* tenth *of-the*-month.

Exercise 10

1. *The* bill *ought-to-be* paid if-*we owe them for-the* wood.
2. May-*we* see-*the* book *which-was to-be given to him*?
3. *We owe him an* apology *for-the* delay *in* mailing-*the* cheque.
4. *We ought to* put-*the* money *in-the* bank. *We-shall do*-so if-*we-can*.
5. May-*we-have a* copy *of-the* bill *for-the* wood we bought *on-the* fifth?
6. *The* name *of-the* book Jessie bought *was* "Making *a* Living."
7. *We-shall go to-the* dock *on*-Monday *to*-take *a* look at-*the* big ship.
8. If-*we-can* get each *of-them to-give* 2s. 6d., *we-shall-have* enough money *to* feed-*the* family *for a* month.
9. *We-think we ought to*-make *an* appeal *for* aid.
10. *Do-we owe him a* fee *for doing-the* job?

Exercise 11

1. If-they *can* get away, they-will *come to* see-*the* game.
2. They-will-*have to*-leave at *two*, if-they *wish to* see *it*.
3. *We-shall-have to* pay *for-the* damage *to-the* boat.
4. Money *for* food *was being given to-the* family monthly.
5. If-*we-can* aid *them in-any*-way, *we ought to-do* so.
6. *It-was too* cool *for* bathing at-*the* beach, so they came back *to-the* pool.
7. They-will-*be* leaving *for* Canada *on-the* tenth *of-the*-month.
8. They-will *go to* Winnipeg *on-the* tenth.
9. *The* lady saw *a* copy *of-the* book "Looking at Asia."
10. If she *can come in to* see us, *we-can* show *the* lady *a* copy *of-the* book *for-which* she-*was* asking.

Exercise 12

1. *We-shall-be* lucky if-*we* get *any* money *for do*ing-*the* job.
2. May*be-the* lunch *can-be given on a different* day.
3. *A* talk *was to-be given on-the* topic "Feeding-*the* Family."
4. Eva *was* talking *of go*ing *to* Manitoba *in* May.
5. If-*they wish to-*make *any* money, they-will-*have to-do-the* job *in a different* way.
6. *The* wood *was too* thick. *It-was an* inch *in* width, so *we-had to* ship *it* back.
7. *We wish to* know if *it-*will make *any difference to-them* if-*we* ship-*the* load *of* coal *to*day.
8. *The* change may-*be put* into effect *in* May.
9. *We-have*-no *wish to-*make *a* change *which*-will affect so-many, *but* they-*have a different* way *of* looking at *it.*
10. If-*we-can think of any-*way *of-do*ing-*the* thing *in a different* way, *we-shall* ask-*them to-come in to* see us.

Exercise 13

1. *To-our* relief, they came early.
2. *We-are* leaving *to*day, *and-we should* reach Winnipeg *in a* day or-*two.*
3. *Who*-will-*be go*ing *to* see-*the* Army *and*-Navy game?
4. If-*we wish to-*get *to-the* game early, *we should-be* ready *in an hour.* Ask Jack *for a* rug.
5. Ray *and* Ruth *are* reading-*the* book "*The* Arm *of-the* Law."
6. *We* wrote *to-them,* asking-*them to-*rush-*the* job, *and*-they say they-will-*have-it* ready *in a* month.
7. *We*-may-*be* wrong, *and-if-we-are, we-shall* readily *give him our* apology.
8. *The* cheque *was put in an* airmail envelope, *and it-should* reach *them to*day.

Exercise 14

1. So far, *we-have-had a* fair share *of* luck.
2. *We-do a* thorough repair job at *our* shop.
3. *We-can* fetch *your* car *and* leave *it* at-*your* door.
4. *We* rang-*the* bell, *but* nobody came *to-the* door.
5. *A year*-ago Jim O'Dair bought-*the* ranch belonging *to-the* Perry family.
6. *The large* ridge at Red Gap *was* rich *in* ore.

7. *It*-will-*be* easy *to*-make *an* error *and* take-*the* wrong road.
8. *We*-fear *we-shall-have to* borrow money if-*we-are to*-carry *on* at-*the* factory.
9. *We should* add enough money *to-the* fee *we give him to* pay *for-the* fare.
10. *The* jury may *think-the* youth *should* get money *for-the* injury.
11. *We-have* thanked him *for-the*-money *we-had to* borrow.
12. They-may *thank-the* judge, *whose* talk *was* put *on-the* air, *for-the* change *in* factory law.

Exercise 15

1. *The* charge *for-the* rug *was* put *on-your* March bill.
2. *We wish to* remove *any* fear they-may-*have*, *and-we-shall* urge *them to* engage *a* lawyer.
3. May-*we* take Polly *and* Jack *to* see-*the* parade *on-the* fourth *of*-March?
4. *We-shall* make-up *a* party *and-have* lunch at-*the* cake shop.
5. *We-are* making *a* tour *of* Italy *in* March.
6. *Our* party *should-be in* Rome *on-the* fourth *of-the*-month.
7. *We-shall* get back *to* Canada *in* May.
8. *The usual* charge *for* parking-*the* car at-*the* garage *was* 2s. 6d.
9. *We* saw *a* copy *of-the* rare book *in-the* shop window.
10. *It-should* pay-*the* firm *to*-go *on-the* air daily.
11. Paul King *was* put *in*-charge *of-the* factory early *in* March.
12. *We-can put a* mark *in* red at-*the* bottom *of*-each page *we* check.

Exercise 16

1. Mary *and* Jack *are to-be* married early *in* March.
2. *We wish to*-go *to-the* wedding, *but* they-may-*be* married *in* Rome, *and it*-will-*be too* far away.
3. *We-shall* ask-*the* lawyer *to*-talk *for an hour*.
4. They-will take *a* lorry load *of* coal *to-the* shop *to*day or *to*morrow.
5. Wrap-*the* package *and* mail *it to*day. *We-think-we ought to* insure-*the* package.
6. *We-have given-them* no authority *to* change-*the* policy *of-the* firm.
7. *We* get *our* milk at-*the* dairy farm, *and-we usually* pay *our* bill monthly.
8. *The* living room *was* at-*the* rear *of-the* shop.

9. *The* door *was too* narrow, *and-we-had to* remove *it to-*get-*the large* package into-*the* room.

10. Mary, *whose* memory *was* poor, read *a different* page *of-the* book each day.

11. *We-can* change-*the* collar *on-the* fur wrap *today, and-the* lady may *come in for-it to*morrow.

Exercise 17

1. *When I-was in-your* shop *on-the* Parade *I-*saw *a different* type *of* tyre tube.

2. *I should* like *to* buy four or five *of-them for-*my car.

3. *I-think-you-*will enjoy *our* show if-*you-can come to* see *it.*

4. *I-wish you to-*make-out *a* cheque *for-the* boiler *and* get *it* off tonight by airmail.

5. *Our* failure *to-do what* they *wish* may annoy *them, but how-can we-do what* they ask?

6. *The* village *was a* mile *beyond-the* mouth *of-the* Wye.

7. *Do-you* know *when* Roy *and* Dinah *are* going *to* Cuba?

8. *I-*know-*the* boy *would* like *to-go with-them.*

9. *Why was-the* charge *put on-*my March bill?

10. *Do-you* know *when-the* ship may leave? *It-*will *go* out *with-the* tide at five.

11. *How* far *do-you have to-*go? *Do-you wish to-come with me?*

12. *You-should* write *your* name *in* ink at-*the* bottom *of-the* form.

Exercise 18

1. *What-do-you think we ought to-do? I-think we should give-them a* month *in-which to* pay-*the* bill.

2. If-*you wish to-*catch-*the* boat, *you-*will-*have to-*leave early.

3. *I-think-you-*will-*have to* buy *a* coil *for-your* car.

4. If-*you-can* arrive at five *you-*will-*be in-*time *for-the* talk.

5. *I-have-*no *wish to* annoy *you, but I-think-the* debt *should-be* paid.

6. *I* admire-*the* type *of* youth *who-*will-*do a* job thoroughly.

7. *For a* low outlay, *you-can* get *a* couch *for-the* room.

8. *A* cure *for-the* lazy boy *would-be to-give him a* job *which-would* keep *him* busy.

9. *Why-have-you* allowed *our* bill *to-*go unpaid?

10. *What-can-we-do for-you?*

11. *You-can* read *and* write *for an hour.*

12. *How-can-we* keep *in-*touch *with-them when-*they *go* away?

13. *Why-do-you think it-would-be-the* wrong *thing to-do?*

14. *I-think-you-are* right, *but-you*-may-*have* to show *why you-are* making-*the* change.

Exercise 19

1. If-*we-are* to pay *our*-way, *we-shall-have* to-get new revenue.
2. *I should* like *to-do what-you* ask, *but I-have*-no power *to-do* so.
3. *It*-will-*be your* duty *to*-check each item *we* charge.
4. *I-shall go to-the* automobile show, *and-I*-may buy *a* new car.
5. *Do-you wish to*-renew *your* fire policy? *It*-will-*be* due *to*morrow.
6. *I*-am-aware *of-the* value *of a* shop window *on-the* avenue.
7. *I*-will *give-you a* cheap rate *to* Niagara via *the* Lake route.
8. *What-would-be your* rate *for a large* room *with* bath or shower?
9. *We-had a* fire, *and our* factory *was* idle *for a* month: so *we-had a* poor *year*.
10. *I-have*-no *wish to* argue *with-you*, *for-you*-may-*be* right *in what-you* say.
11. *You*-will rub *your* eyes *when-you* see *our* New Era car.
12. *Why are-you* buying *a* poor type *of* oil *when-you can* get *a* pure oil *for-your* money?
13. Poor oil may damage *your* car; *it*-will pay *you* to buy *a* purer variety.

Exercise 20

Would-you like *to*-go *to* America *with me in*-July? *I*-know *you*-will thoroughly enjoy-*the* tour if-*you-can come with me*. *I*-am-*going with a* jolly party *of* four or five, *and-we-are* making *a* tour *which*-will take *a* month.

We-are leaving *on-the* S.S. Canada *on-the* fifth *of*-July, *and-we-are* due *to* arrive *in* America *on-the* tenth. *We-can* get *a* cheap rate *for-the* voyage if-*we* share *a* room *on-the* boat.

Write *to-me in a* day or-*two and* say *you*-will *come*. (99)

Exercise 21

Do-you think-you-will-*be* rich enough *to*-retire *when-you* reach-*the* age *of* fifty? *You*-will-*be* rich if-*you-can* retire *with* enough money *to*-live *on*. *We-can* show *you how you-can* buy *a* life annuity *for a* low outlay now.

How would your family fare if-*you-should* die now? *Can-you* leave enough *for-them to*-live *on*?

We-are-now issuing *a* new life policy *which*-will make-*it* easy *for-you*

to-do what-you would wish. *You-can* take-out-*the* policy *for a* low charge. *We*-know *you*-will like *it.* *Would-you* like *to* see *it*?
If so, write *your* date *of* birth below *and* mail-*the* form *to*day.   (122)

Exercise 22

1. *I-have* many *a* happy memory *of-the* time *of*-my youth *on-the* farm.
2. *I*-saw-*the* buyer *for a* minute at-*the* hotel, *but* he *had to* hurry away.
3. *Usually we* ship-*the* oil *to-you* by boat, *but* if-*you-are in a* hurry, *it can go* by road.
4. Write *and* ask-*them* if-they charge *a* higher rate *for* heavy oil.
5. They hope *to-have-the* bill *of*-lading *in-the* mail *to*day.
6. *I*-know Hugh Riley, *and-I-think-he*-will reach *a* high rank *in-the* army.
7. *We*-hope-*you*-will enjoy-*the* voyage, *and-we*-hope *to* see-*you when-you* get back.

Exercise 23

I should like-*the* head *of-your* firm *to* see *our* huge new factory, *and*-if-*he*-will *come, I*-will fetch *him in*-my car. If-*he-can do*-so, *I should* like *him to-have* lunch *with me* at-*the* Park Avenue Hotel.

I-hope he-will *come to* see *it, for I-think-it*-will appeal *to him.* *I-shall-be* happy *to* see *him, and you,* if-*you-can come too.* *I*-hope-*you*-will *come with him.*   (82)

Exercise 24

1. *We-have-your* message, *and-we-shall-have-the* invoice *and-the* bills *of*-lading ready by-*the* time *the* ship sails *on*-Wednesday.
2. Since-*the* business *for-the-year* shows *a* heavy loss, *the* bank may wish *to-have a* voice *in-the* firm's affairs.
3. *We* refuse *to* pay *this* sum, *when-we-can* get-*the* same items *for* less.
4. May-*we*-know *why this* small bill *is* unpaid? *As you* know, *we-have* allowed *it to*-go *beyond-the usual* time. *We-shall-be* happy *to-give-you* details *of any of-the* items *which* appear *on-the* bill.
5. *In a* month, *we*-hope *to* add-*the* names *of a* dozen firms *which*-will sell *our* silk.
6. *I-have*-seen-*the* head *of-the* firm, *and-I-think-he*-will renew-*the* lease *on-the* office *in* South Avenue.
7. He-will, *I-think,* wish *to*-lease fewer rooms *and-thus* effect *a* saving.

8. *His* firm *has had a* poor *year, and-for-this*-reason he *has to*-save some money.
9. *We-shall-be* happy *to-give-you-the* names *of-those* hotels *which have* bought *them*.

Exercise 25

We-are happy *to* announce *a* sale *of-the* famous Arch Form shoes. *The* factory *is* anxious *to-have* many new buyers *for*-these shoes, *and-for-this*-reason *is* selling *them to-the* dealers *for* less *this* month.
We-hope-*you*-will *come in* soon. *When-you* see-*the* shoes *we-think-you*-will *wish to*-select *several* pairs, *and*-if-*you do*-so *you*-will effect *a large* saving. *We*-know *of* no similar value. *We-have-them in-any* size. Each pair *has-the usual* guarantee *of-the* factory.
We advise *you to-come in* early, *for* if-*you* delay *you*-may miss some *of-the* value *of-the* sale.   (113)

Exercise 26

1. *We-have a* nice house *for* sale *in* Rose Park. *It-has* six rooms *and two* baths.
2. *We-have* sold twice *as* many copies *of-the* book since-*the* notice *was* put *in-the*-magazine.
3. Now *is-the* time *to* buy *your* bulbs *and* seeds. *The* soil *is* ready *for-them*.
4. *We-have* many choice varieties *on* sale, *and-we*-hope-*you*-will *come in and* choose some.
5. He said-*the* city *would-have to*-raise *the* oil tax or else levy *a* sales tax.
6. *I-shall-be in-your* city *on* Tuesday, 20th-March, *and-I should* like *to-speak to-you*, if-*you-can* spare *a* few minutes.
7. *I*-am leaving-*the* city *on* Tuesday. *I-shall-be* sorry *to*-miss *you, but I-have*-no choice.
8. *Our* cashier daily takes-*the* cheques *which come in-the*-mail *to-the* bank.
9. Bill *has to* pay-*the* cheque into-*the* bank *on*-Saturday *when-he* leaves-*the* office.
10. *On*-Saturday *we-are hav*ing *a special* sale *of* boys' suits.

Exercise 27

1. My book, *which*-will-*be* ready soon, *gives* my views *on-the subject* "*The* Music *of-our* Times."

2. *I*-hope *to-give a* series *of*-talks *in several different* cities, *and-I-have* chosen *this subject for*-my talks.
3. If *I*-write out-*the* names *of-the* cities *and-the* dates *on which I*-am *to-speak, can-you* type-*the* schedule *for-me*? *I should* like *to-have two* copies.
4. *I-shall-be* happy if-*you*-will type *a* copy *of*-my speech *for-me*. *It-is* forty pages *in* length.
5. *How*-long does *it* take *to* type such *a* long speech? *Can-you have-it* ready *for-me in two hours*?
6. *The* head *of-the* firm said, "*I*-am *going to-give-you a* higher salary *because of-the* absence *of* errors *in-the* jobs *I-have given-you to-do*."
7. *Thank-you for-your* news. Many *thanks, too, for-the*-magazines. *I*-am happy *to* know *you-are hav*ing *a* nice time.
8. *I*-enjoy reading *two special* items *in-the*-magazine: "*The* Way *Things* Seem *to-Me*" and "News Outside-*the* Door."
9. *We owe several large* items *on-this* month's bills *which ought to-be* paid *in a* few days.
10. May-*we*-know soon *what-you* decide *to-do*? *What-would-be-the* wise *thing to-do*?

Exercise 28

1. *We wish to-be of* service *to-you, and-we-shall-be* happy *to* change-*the* shoes if-*you*-will mail *them to*-us.
2. May-*we*-know *when you*-will-*have-the* new designs *for-the* ladies' suits ready *for*-us?
3. *What-is-the* cause *of-the* delay? *You* seem *to-be* slow *in* making *them* up.
4. *You*-will receive *them in a* few days. *We*-hope-*you*-will excuse-*the* delay.
5. *We-are* slow *because of-our* desire *to-give-you* designs *which-*will-*be different and* new, *and it* takes many *hours to*-make *them*.
6. *We* highly value-*the* share *of-your* business *which-you have given*-us *for-several years*.
7. *In-the* face *of*-these facts, *we-think-you-are* wrong *in* passing *on-the* charges *to*-us.
8. Thomas *wishes to*-go *with*-us *to-the* baseball game *on*-Saturday. If-*he-goes with*-us he-will take-us *in-his* car.
9. *When is-the* summary *of-which-you speak to-be* ready?
10. Samuel Johnson, *whose* speech appears *in to*day's "News," *speaks* tonight at-*the* Academy. *What-is his subject*?

11. *His* topic *is* "Signs *of-the* Times." *I-think-he usually speaks on-several subjects.*
12. James Smith *thinks-the* firm charge *too* high *a* fee *for*-these maps.
13. They charge-us 5 guineas *a* set, *and* he *thinks we-can* get *them for* less.
14. He-will show-us *how we-can* secure *them for* 4 guineas *a* set *and-thus* save *a* guinea.
15. *What-is-the* size *of-the* box? *It-is* six-inches wide *and*-five inches deep.
16. *I* use *it for-the* purpose *of*-saving odd pennies.

Exercise 29

1. *When-we* insure *a* package *which-we* dispatch by-mail, *do-we* get *a* receipt?
2. *A* zeal *for* justice *should-be-the* mark *of*-each citizen, high or low, rich or poor.
3. *We* readily obey laws *which* history teaches *are-the* wisdom *of*-centuries.
4. *We-have-several large* desks *which-we* wish *to* dispose *of*. *I-think-we* should reduce *them to* 6 guineas apiece, *and*-if-*we do*-so, *we ought to* succeed *in* disposing *of-them*.
   Besides-*the* desks, *we-have-several large* red rugs *which-we-have-had in-the* shop *too*-long, *and-I-think-we ought to put them on* sale, *too*. If-*we* make-*them* cheap enough, *we should-have* many customers *for-them*. *What-do-you think?*
   I-wish-you would-come to-the city *and* discuss *this* sale *with*-us. (91)

Exercise 30

1. *I-wish to* cancel my passage *on-the* vessel sailing *on* 16th-March.
2. *The* judge's counsel *is* wise *and* sincere, *and-I-think-we should* listen *to what-he*-says.
3. *I*-will write *to an* officer *of-the* firm *to*day, *and-when I* receive *an* answer *I*-will get *in*-touch *with-you*.
4. *When-you* know these lessons thoroughly, *you*-will-*be on-your* way *to a* business career.

Exercise 31

1. *It*-will assist *me* if-*you*-will make-up *an* itemized list *of all-the* stock *we-have in-the* store.
2. *The* list *should* also state-*the* cost *of*-each item.
3. *Although our* costs *are* high, *we-have al*ways refused *to*-lessen-*the* value *of-our* service.

4. Honest value assists *our* firm *to*-keep *its* customers, *and* also *to* secure new buyers.
5. *Our* silk may-*be subjected to any* test *you*-may *wish to*-make.
6. *We-think your first* step *should-be to* stop waste *as*-fast-*as you-can. We*-suggest adjusting *your* charges *as-the next* step.
7. *Our* sales *this year al*ready exceed *all of-our* sales *for* last *year.*
8. *Although you* invoiced *the* steel posts *to*-us last month, *we-are* still *hav*ing *to*-make *do with* stone posts.
9. *Your* failure *to*-get *them to*-us *on* time *has* caused *a* big upset *in-the* schedule, *and-has* cost *a large* sum *of*-money.
10. *We-shall-do* our best *to influence him to* cancel *the* debt.
11. *In-the* past *we-have* used *this* style *of* pencil, *and-we*-know *it*-will-*be all*-right *for-your* purpose.
12. *Almost all* types *of* stencils *have a* mark *to* show *when-you* reach-*the* bottom *of-the* page.

Exercise 32

1. *It-is-the* type *of* stock *which-should* appeal *to* small investors, *and-the* bank *has* advised many *of-its* customers *to* invest some money *in-the* issue.
2. *I-*am *always influenced* by-*the* bank's advice, *and-I-have-had* no reason *to-be* sorry.
3. *When-you* master *this subject, you*-will-*have a* tool *which*-will assist *you to* secure *a* post *in a* business office.
4. *When-do-you think-you*-will-*have-the large* posters ready *for*-us? *We wish to*-mail *them to-the different* stores *on-our* list.
5. *The* Webster Hotel *is-the* finest *in* Chester, *and-we*-hope-*you*-will register at-*this* hotel *when-you come to-our* city.
6. *The* steamer leaves *on*-Wednesday, *the* sixth *of-the*-month, *and-we*-must know by-*the first* if-*you wish to* ship-*the* coffee by-*this* boat.
7. *We-have-had-the* case *of* books *in-the* customs office *for almost a* month. *What-is-the* charge *for* storage?
8. Each *year,* research shows *how to*-make *things* faster *and-with* less toil. *What are-we do*ing *with-the* time *we* save?
9. *The* loss caused by unpaid bills *is-the* smallest *we-have-had in several years.*

Exercise 33

1. *The* heavy losses *which-the* firm *has to* absorb *this year are almost* enough *to*-exhaust *its* resources.
2. *The* firm *has had a* series *of* poor *years. Do-you* know-*the* causes *of*-these successive losses?

3. *The* firm *itself gives several* reasons. Among-*them are-the* steady rise *in* costs *and* higher taxes.
4. *What-is-the* basis *for-your* appeal *to-have your* state taxes reduced?
5. *I-am-sorry to-*lose *your* services, *but, as I-have al*ready said, *you have* my best *wishes for-your* success. *I-shall al*ways-*be* happy *to-*receive news *of-your do*ings.
6. *Our* pipes *are* nicely boxed, *and-we-*know *it-*will pay *you to put* some *of-them in-your* showcases or *in-your* windows.
7. *We-have to-*make *a* small charge *for-the* boxes, *but-the* pipes sell *much* faster *when-you* show *them in-the* boxes.
8. "*The* Times" successfully appeals each *year for* money *for* needy cases, *and it* raises *a large* sum *for-the* purposes *of* charity. Aid *is-as* necessary *this year as-in-the* past.
9. *I-think-the* charges *for-*these posters *are* excessive, *and-I-wish* to satisfy *myself of-the* necessity *for-the* high fees paid *to-the* artists.
10. If-*you* insist, *we-shall* pay-*the* fees *ourselves, but-the* artists *themselves think-the* charges *are* low *for-this* type *of* job.

Exercise 34

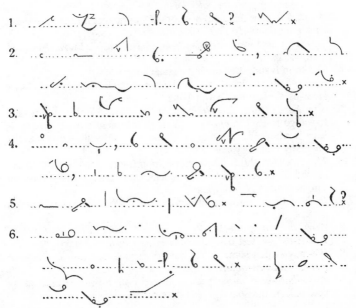

7. [shorthand outline] x [shorthand outline] x

8. [shorthand outline]

[shorthand outline] x

9. [shorthand outline] x

10. [shorthand outline]

[shorthand outline] x

Exercise 35

1. May-*we-have* *as*-soon-*as*-possible *the* cases *of* Swan Soap *which-you-are* making-up *specially for*-us?

2. *We wish to-have this* soap *as*-soon-*as you-can* get *it to*-us, *as-we-are* having *a* sale *on-the first of-the* month.

3. *This-is an* item *which-we wish to*-emphasize, *as-we*-know *it*-will sell readily.

4. *The* swan *is* supposed *to*-sing *a* sweet song *when-it-is* dying. *This-is* said *to-be-the* sweetest song *it* sings, *and-this-is-the* story *which-has given*-us *the* famous "Swan Song."

5. *New-York is-the largest* city *in-the United-States-of*-America. *If-you*-go *to-the* top *of any of-the* high towers *of-this*-city, *you*-will-have *a* view *which* takes *in all-the* city *as-well-as-the* suburbs *for*-many miles *beyond*.

6. *The* monster ships *which come to this*-city dot-*the* bay. They unload huge cargoes *on-the* docks, *and* take away *with-them* similar loads *when*-they leave.

7. *In-this*-city *the* business life *of-the United-States* reaches *its* high peak.

8. *As-we-are go*ing *to-the* docks, *we-can* look at-*the* new vessel. *This-is-the* swiftest *as*-well-*as-the largest of-the* steamers.

9. *We*-may switch some *of-our* business *to-the* new firm *as-they-will give*-us value *as-well-as* service.

10. *As-we-have*-seen *in-the* past, *a* heavy poll *usually* sweeps many new officers into-*the different* state offices.

Exercise 36

1. *When can-you* ship-*the* acid *you* sold *to*-us last month? *We-are as* busy *as-we-can-be* just-now, *and-the* delay *is* causing *much* annoyance *to-our* customers *as*-well-*as* loss *to-ourselves.* (38)
2. *You-can* rely *on* receiving-*the* acid *in two*-days. *It*-will leave *this*-city *tomorrow and-we* assume *it*-will reach-*you the next* day. *We*-must apologize *for-the* delay. *Owing to-the* heavy losses caused by-*the* fire at *our* factory last month *our* stocks became *too*-low. *We-are* making-up *for* lost time *as*-fast-*as we-can.* (63)

Exercise 37

*We-are hav*ing *a special* sale *of-our* essences, *as-it-is*-necessary *to* dispose *of*-some *of-our* stock *as*-early-*as*-possible. *How*-much *shall we* set aside *for-you*? *As-we*-know just *what you-can* use, *we-can,* if-*you*-like, select *a* dozen cases, *and you-can* take-*them as*-soon-*as you-are* ready. (60)

Exercise 38

We-fear-*the* cost *of-your* steel fences *is too* high. *Although-we-have* bought *them* each season *for-the* past six *years, we-think-we-shall* lose business *because-we-have to*-charge *too*-much *for-them.*
In-this-city *we*-must sell at low rates if-*we-are to*-make *a* success *of-our* business. *Owing to-this* fact, *we-have to*-emphasize-*the* necessity *of*-reducing *as-much-as*-possible *the* costs *to-our* customers. *Can-you* suggest *something which*-will assist us? (86)

Exercise 39

1. *I-wish to-do something to* assist *young* Jackson. *Can-you do anything to* induce *him to*-make *a* thorough study *of-the language*? *I*-know *you*-will-*be* ready *to* assist *him as-much-as*-possible, *and-I*-know he-will-*be influenced* by-*your* advice. (47)
2. *Inasmuch-as it-is*-necessary *in-this-subject to*-deal extensively *with-the language,* he-*should* see *how* easy *it-is to* study *as*-far-*as*-possible such *things as* style *and-the* best usage. Nowadays business houses set *an especially* high value *on-the* ability *to* use *the language in-the* right way. *Because* so-much emphasis *is*-now *given to-this* ability, he-*should* resolve *to*-make *himself as*-far-*as*-possible *a* master *of-the* best form. Now *his language* sense *is* poor, *but-when-he* knows *how*-much *it*-may affect *his* career, *I*-know he-will-*do all* he-*can to* remedy *as*-soon-*as*-possible *the* errors he-makes. (115)

2

Exercise 40

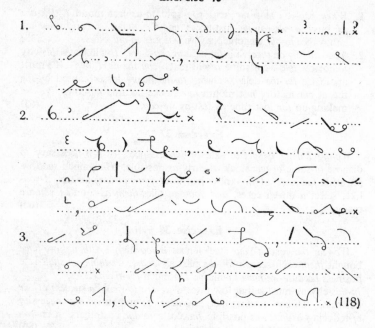

1.

2.

3.

× (118)

Exercise 41

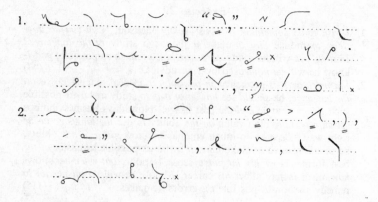

1.

2.

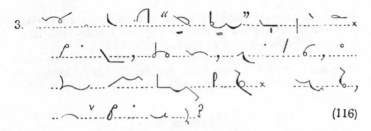

(116)

Exercise 42

1. *When I*-left *New-York I*-asked *to-have* my mail *sent on to-me* at Winnipeg. *Although I-shall-be in* Winnipeg *on*-Wednesday, *the* 16th, *I*-may *go on to* Regina late *that* night.
2. *In-any-*case, *I should-be in* Regina *on-the* 17th, *and-I-think it-would-be* best *to* dispatch my mail *to-that* city, *as-it*-might not reach Winnipeg *in*-time.
3. *The* York Store *could*-not *give-me a* cheque *as you wished.* They said-*the* best they *could-do would-be to* pay *in two*-months' time.
4. *I could-do nothing with-them* at-*this*-time. *The* firm *is* moving *its* store *to* Baxter Avenue, *and-for-that* reason *I-could*-not sell *them anything.* They-will let-*me*-know *as-*soon-*as-the* new store *is* ready.

Exercise 43

*We-are-*sorry *to* know *that-the-*goods *we* charged *on-our* invoice *of* 10th August *have*-not-yet reached-*you. We* shipped *them in two* cases *the* same day *the* bill *was* sent *to-you, and-we* marked *and* shipped *the* cases *in-the* usual way.
*As-*far-*as we*-know, *the* cases *should* reach-*you as-*soon-*as-this* note, *that-is, to*day or *to*morrow. (67)

Exercise 44

1. *We-have* issued *a* booklet *which gives* details *of-the* new automatic toaster *we-have*-just *put on-the* market. *You-can* secure *a* copy *of-this* booklet *as-*well-*as our* latest catalogue by writing *for-them. We* make absolutely no charge.
2. *I-have* submitted *an* estimate *for* do*ing-the* job, *but-*they *have*-not-yet notified *me that-*they-will accept my bid.
3. *This* item *is* listed *in-the* catalogue at 4 guineas. If-*you* remit *in* five days *you-can* deduct *two* per-cent.

4. *We-have*-not-yet received-*the* goods invoiced by-*you on* 4th-May. *We*-hope *that-you*-will get *them* to-us by *next* Tuesday at-*the* latest, *as-we-are quite out of* stock *of*-some *of*-these items.
5. *Why has-the* firm kept us waiting *for-the* steel sheets? They stated *in a* recent note *that-the* sheets *had* actually left-*the* factory. If-they did ship *them when*-they said, *the* sheets *should-have* arrived by now.

Exercise 45

We-are-sorry *that-you-could*-not use *the* stockings *we-sent-you a* few days ago. *Our* stock *of-the* exact shade *you* specified *was* exhausted, so *we-sent* instead *a* similar shade *and* style. *We-had* no-doubt *that-you could* use *them, but-we should*-not-*have* shipped *them without first* writing *to-you*.
If-*you wish*, they-may-*be sent* back *to*-us, *and-we-shall* cancel *the* charge. (73)

Exercise 46

*We-are hav*ing *a* benefit show *next* Wednesday night, *and-I*-am-writing *to* invite *you* to-come. Aid *is* badly needed *for*-some *special* cases *we-have on-our* list, *and-all-the* money *is-to-be* used *for-that* purpose.
The cost *of-the* tickets *is* 3s. 6d. each. *I*-know-*that-you*-will *wish to* assist *the* cause *as-much-as*-possible, *and-that-you*-will let-*me-have your* cheque *for-several* tickets. (79)

Exercise 47

The attached sheet shows-*the* result *of-the-year's* business. *You*-will-note-*that*, except *for-the first two*-months, business *for-the-year was* good. *We* adopted *a* new sales policy *in* March, *and* since *that*-time *we-have* enjoyed *the* benefit *of-our* new methods. *We-have-had* about twice *as*-many sales *as-in-the* same-months last-*year*. *We-think that-this-is-the* best evidence *we could-have of-the* value *of-our* new policy. (80)

Exercise 48

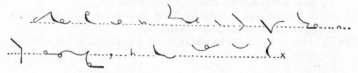

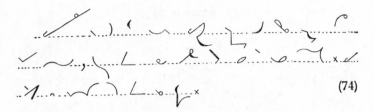

(74)

Exercise 49

We-are-sorry *that-you*-received *in* error *a* cheque intended *for* Reed *and*-Sons *of* Edinburgh. *Thank-you for* passing *it to*-us.
We-are writing *to*day *to* Reed *and*-Sons asking-*them to*-let *you* have-*the* cheque *which-we should-have* sent *to-you*. No-doubt *you*-will receive *it without*-delay. (55)

Exercise 50

I-am happy *to* say *that-the* cut *in* rates about *which I* wrote *to-you in* March *is*-now *to-be put* into effect. *I-think-that-the* rate *on-your* house *is subject to* change *on-the* new basis.
Your policy *should-be sent to-this* office *as*-soon-*as*-possible, so-*that you*-may-*have-the* benefit *of-the* reduced rate. (64)

Exercise 51

We-have looked *for a* small house *for-you*, *and-we-think we-have*-just *the* house *you*-will *wish to* buy. *It-has* six nice rooms *and two* baths. *The* lot *is* large, *and-the* house *is* so located *that* each room *has a* lovely view. *We-think you-could*-not buy *a* house *in a* nicer spot.
If-*you*-like *we-can* go out *to* see *it* tonight. *It*-will take-us about forty minutes by car *to*-get *to* Meadow Park. (84)

Exercise 52

*We-have-sent to-you to*day *a* copy *of-our* latest catalogue *as*-well-*as* some *special* booklets *which-we-think-you*-will like *to-have*. When *any* new designs *are* issued *we-shall* post details *to-you* so-*that-you*-will-*be* up *to-the* minute.
As-far-*as we*-know, these designs *are*-not stocked by *any*body else *in-your* territory, *and*-no-doubt they will-*be* popular *with your* customers. (73)

Exercise 53

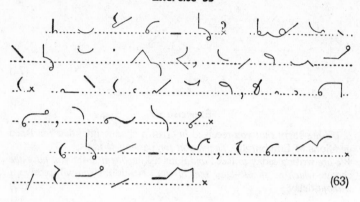

(63)

Exercise 54

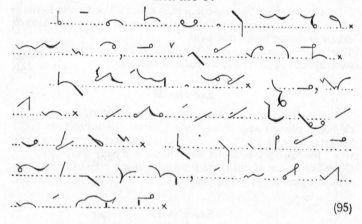

(95)

Exercise 55

1. Until *quite* recently *the* volume *of-our* business *in-the* south *was* *quite* small, *but* since last *November we-have-had an* office *in* Fulham, *and-the* volume *of-*sales *has* risen steadily.
2. Sales *in-this* territory *for January and-February are-the* best *in-the* history *of-the* firm.

3. *In*-these *two*-months *we-have* sold twice *as-much in-the* south *as we* sold last-*year*.
4. *The* fact *that-this-is* almost *as-much-as we-have* sold *in* Manchester shows *that our* new policy *is* entirely justified.
5. *We*-feel *that-the*-result *of-our* new policy *is most satisfactory*.
6. *The* race *is*-not *always to-the* swift. Sometimes *too*-much haste makes *for* less speed.
7. *Never* waste time by *having to-do-the*-same job twice. *This-is* useful advice, *and*-if-*you*-will follow *it*, *it*-will assist *you to-be* successful.
8. Write *your* notes accurately *and* neatly, so-*that* not-only *you*, *but* *any*body else, *can* read *them* easily.

Exercise 56

Recently *we* wrote *to-you and* stated *that*, unless *we* received *your* cheque by 16th *February*, *we should-have to* ask *our* lawyer *to*-take steps *to* force *you to* pay-*the* bill *you owe* us. Unfortunately *you have*-not answered *our* note, *and*-now *we*-must *inform-you that-we-have* asked *our* lawyer *to*-go ahead *and*-follow-*the usual* methods *to*-make *you* pay.
We-are exceedingly sorry *to-have to-do* so, *but*, evidently *this-is-the* only way *in-which we-can* secure *our* money. *We* certainly feel *that-we-have* acted *quite* fairly *with-you, and, as-we-have*-said, *this* seems *to-be-the* only *thing* left *for*-us *to-do*.
If-*you* mail *your* cheque *without-the* slightest delay, *you-can* avoid heavy costs, *and-we* advise *you to-do* so *as*-soon-*as you*-receive *this*. (145)

Exercise 57

I-think that-the way *in-which we* store goods at-*the* factory *is*-not *altogether satisfactory*. *It*-seems *to-me that-the* fire *insurance* rates *are*-now *quite* high, *and-I*-feel *that*, *with* some changes *in-the* store-rooms, reduced rates might *be expected*.
I should like *you to inspect-the* rooms *as*-soon-*as*-possible, *and*-if, *as a* result *of-your* inspection, *you think that our* methods *with respect to-the* storage *of*-goods *are* un*satisfactory*, *I-wish you would* suggest *any* changes *which could-be put* into effect.
I-wish you would let-*me-have-the different insurance* policies now *in* force, *together-with-the* details *of-the* scale *on-which-the insurance* rates *are* based, so-*that I-can* make *an* analysis *of-the* annual cost. (132)

Exercise 58

1. *I-shall* arrive at 10 a.m. *on* Tuesday, 12th-*January*, unless *I-have* to-make *a* change. *I*-will wire *you* if-*the* time *is* changed.
2. *As*-far-*as* I-am-aware, *the* goods were dispatched at-least *a* week ago. *I*-will look into *this and give-you-the* exact date they-were *sent*.
3. Allen *and* Royal *have* built up *a* nice business *for-themselves in* Nelson. *The* success *of-the* business *is* due entirely *to-the* way *in-which* they-*have* worked.
4. *A* few *years*-ago they-were *quite* poor, *but* now both *of-them are* worth *a large* sum *of*-money.
5. *What-is-the* reason *for-the* higher *insurance* rates *which*-were *put* into effect last week? *The* rise *was quite* un*expected*.
6. *This* state *of* affairs existed *for a* long-time, despite-*the* fact *that-we*-were-not satisfied *with-it*.
7. *We*-were amused at many *things* he said, *but* he-*was* certainly worth listening *to*.
8. He said, "*You*-may die *young because of* worry, *but* certainly work *never* caused-*the* death *of any*body."
9. *Thank-you for-your* note *in-which-you* stated *that-you*-were desirous *of-having an* agency *for-the* sale *of-our* textiles *in-your* city.
10. *We-have never given any* firm *the* sole right *to*-sell *our* goods, *and-this* policy does-not allow us *to-give-you-the* sole agency. *We should-be* happy *to-have-you* retail *our* goods *and-we*-hope-*you*-will *do*-so at-*the usual* dealers' rates.

Exercise 59

When may-*we expect-the two* dozen barrels *of*-lime *which*-were *to-be* shipped *the first* week *in February*? Unless *we* receive-*the* lime *this* week *we-shall-have to* cease work *on-the* new road at Elm Park.
We-thought *we could* rely *on having-the* lime last week *without* fail, *and your* failure *to*-get *it to*-us *is most* unfortunate. *We*-hope *that-the* barrels *are on-the* way, *and-that-you-can* wire-us *that-we*-may *expect them to*morrow.
(85)

Exercise 60

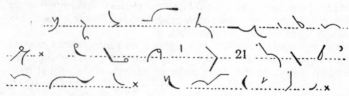

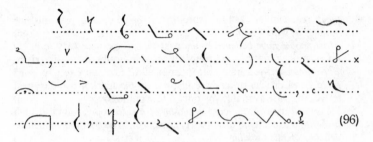

(96)

Exercise 61

1. *This* simple device saves *you* many *hours of* toil. Just fill *in-the* attached form below *and* post *it* *to*-us, or apply *to-your* local dealer *for* details *of-this* useful article. (33)

2. Please supply *me with a* few samples *of*-cloth *in* blue *and* black, *which-would-be* suitable *for* autumn suits. *I should-be*-obliged if-*you would* include *a* couple *of*-samples each *of* single *and* double widths. (39)

3. Please *deliver to*-us *as*-early-*as*-possible fifty copies *of-the* book entitled "Clothes *and How to*-Make-*Them.*" These-*are to-be* supplied at *a* total cost *of* 20 guineas, including *delivery*. (34)

4. *We-are*-pleased *to* know *that-you*-will-*be*-able-*to deliver* some *of-the* tables by-*the first of-January, and-that-you expect to* supply-*the* rest *in two* weeks. *We-shall-be*-obliged if-*you*-will get enough *to*-us by-*the first to* enable-us *to*-make *a special* display *of-them*. (56)

5. *I-believe that* many *of-the* articles *in-this* sale *should-be especially* valuable *to-you*. *For-the first* time *in-the* history *of-the* store, *we-are* able-*to*-make-*them* available at *a* reasonably low cost, *and-I* urge *you to-call and-inspect* them *as*-soon-*as you* possibly *can*. *Do* not wait *till it-is too*-late. (61)

Exercise 62

1. *I called-the* house *several*-times, *and-inasmuch-as* each time *I-was* unable *to*-get *any* reply, *I-think that*-these *people* were away *and-the* house *was* closed. (30)

2. *You have*-not replied *to-our* note *of* 4th *February* asking *for a* cheque *for-the*-goods supplied *to-you* on 12th-*November*. *We would* like *to* know *why you have*-not settled *this*-bill. (35)

3. If-*you wish to*-place *your* furs *in cold* storage *we-can* call *for-them and deliver-them to-you when-you tell*-us *to do*-so. *Our* charges *are*

most reasonable. Let-us store *them for-you, and you*-will-*have nothing to* worry about. (46)

4. *Most people have believed in-the* past *that-it-was*-necessary *to* pay *a* lot *of*-money *for a* good club settee. No-doubt they-were right. *But-we-can tell-you* now *that-it-is*-not at-*all* necessary *to* pay *much for a* good article, *as-we-have* just *put on-the* market *our* Easy-rest settee, *which-is* available *for* only *a* few guineas. (66)

5. Please *tell*-us *what-the* cost *would-be of a* safe about four feet high *and-with a* capacity *of* about forty cubic feet. *The* cost *should* include *delivery to-this building*. (32)

Exercise 63

In-the belief that-you-will *wish to* stop at *a* simple *but* pleasant hotel, *we-have-sent to-you to*day *a* copy *of-our* recently issued booklet.

The total charge *for a* couple per week *is* only 10 guineas. *This* rate includes *a* double room. Single rooms *are* 5 guineas *and* up. *Our* fare *is* simple *but* good. *People tell*-us *that our* table *is first*-class. They say, indeed, *that-it-has*-no *equal. We* doubt *that-it-is* un*equalled, but-we-do* know *that-we* use only *the* best foods *and-that our* charges *are quite* reasonable. *We* make no charge at-*all for* golf or swimming. (111)

Exercise 64

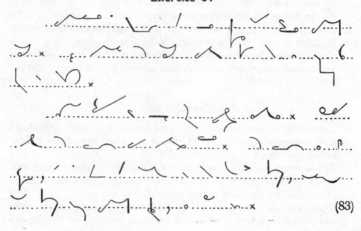

(83)

Exercise 65

1. *This* newspaper tries *to*-bring *to-its* readers *the truth and nothing but-the truth.*

2. *We-are*-sorry *to-have to* trouble *you, but-we* notice *that-you have* charged £22 10s. 6d. *for-your* catalogue item *number* 463 *which-you* supplied *to*-us *on* 16th October. *In-your* price-list *the* item *is* listed at £21 10s. 6d. *A* credit *of* £1 *is thus* due *to*-us. *This-is* evidently *an* error *in* billing. (70)

3. *Thank-you for* bringing *to-our* notice *the* error *in-the* bill *of* 16th October *for* four oak *chairs. We-are*-enclosing *our* credit note *for* £1, *and-we* apologize *for-the* trouble *to-which we-have put you.* (40)

4. *Dear*-Sir, *We-are*-glad *to* know *that-you* wish *to-be a member of-our* club. *As* manager *of-the* club, *I-wish you to* feel at *liberty to* use *our* facilities until *you-are* elected *a member. Your* name *is-to-be* proposed *next* week. *Yours*-truly, (49)

Exercise 66

Dear-Sirs, *During-the* month *of*-April *we*-propose *to* increase-*the* prices *of a number of-the* items at-present *in-the* catalogue. *The* increases *are* necessary *because-of-the* higher costs *we* now *have to* absorb. If-*your* branch *is* going *to* issue *a* new catalogue, *you-should*-not proceed *with-it* until *you have-the* new prices.

Please *remember that-you*-must not issue *your* list until *we* post *you the* new prices. *Yours*-truly, (79)

Exercise 67

Dear Miss Black, *In* April *we* brought out *a* new series *of* history books. *The* series *is for* use *in* forms *two to* six. These-books solve many problems *for-the* teacher. They treat *the subject in a* bright, practical way, *and-we-think-you*-will-agree-*that-the* series *gives a* new *and* better approach *to-the subject.*

With your present heavy programme, *the* books *should* enable-*you to*-make-*the* greatest progress *with your* classes. If-*you would care to* inspect-*the* books, *we* *should-be*-glad *to* dispatch copies *to-you.* If-*you would give-the* books *a* trial, *we*-know *you would-be* delighted *with-the*-results. *Yours*-truly, (113)

Exercise 68

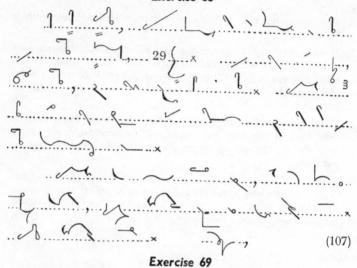

(107)

Exercise 69

1. *This* paper *is* extremely strong. *Its* extra strength makes *it especially* suitable *for-your* purpose.
2. *I-am-sorry to-have to* disagree *with-you, but I-believe that-it-would-be* best *to*-make-out *a* separate bill *for*-each item *delivered.*
3. *The* duties *of a* good secretary *are* described *in-this* book. Each duty *is* set out separately, *and* fully discussed. *I-believe that-this*-book *would-be most* useful *to-you.*
4. *Our* catalogue describes-*the different* items fully. *You*-will-note-*that* each item *is given a* separate *number.*
5. *I-believe that a large-number of-the members of-our* society were *surprised and* displeased at-*the* extreme views presented by-*the* speaker *in-his* address *on "The Liberty of-the* Press."

Exercise 70

Dear-Sirs, *We*-enclose *a description of-the building in* Spring Street. *We-think-this building is an* extremely valuable piece *of*-property, *and-we* strongly urge *you to* buy *it. It-is* quite close *to-the* new south road. *You-can* buy *it today for a* small outlay, *and-we-have*-no-doubt *that in a* few *years it*-will increase *in*-value. *We-believe in*-fact *that in a year* or-*two* property *in-this* district *should-be* worth double *its* present price. *Why* not *inspect it as*-soon-*as you* possibly *can? Yours*-truly, (97)

Exercise 71

1. *Our* records show *that-you have*-not purchased *anything in-this* store *for*-some-time. *We* regard *this as most* unfortunate, *for-we* value *your* patronage highly. *We*-hope *that-it-is*-not due *to*-some un*satisfactory* purchase or *to*-some lack *of* proper service. *We wish to-give-you* service strictly *in*-accordance *with your* desires. (57)
2. *Several members of-the* college faculty expressed *the belief that-it-was* absolutely necessary *to* include *an* extra course *in-this-subject.*
3. *Our* industry prospers *because-of-the* direct methods *we* employ *with our* customers. *We tell-them* only *the truth when-we* describe *our* products.
4. *I-think-that-we* should take-*the* proper steps *to*-bring-about-*the* passage *of*-these bills relating *to*-labour problems, *and I-believe-that care should-be* exercised by-*all* not *to* obstruct *this.*
5. *It-is equally* true *that-the* recent decreases *in-the* prices *of* cheaper fabrics *are expected to*-result *in* increased sales.

Exercise 72

Dear-Sir, *I-shall-be much*-obliged if-*you*-will supply *me with a* few samples *of* extra strong "super" glazed paper, such-*as would-be* suitable *for*-my class *of* work. *The* colours *I most* desire *to* see *are* dark blue *and* grey.

If-*the* samples satisfy *me, and-the* prices *and* terms *of*-sale *are* reasonable, *I-believe I-shall-be* able-*to*-deal extensively *with-you.*

I-shall-be-pleased if-*you*-will also include *in-the* parcel *a* sample or-*two of a* stouter make *of* paper. *I should* like *to*-receive these samples by Wednesday, if-possible. *Yours*-truly, (104)

Exercise 73

Dear-Sirs, *We-are*-pleased *to-tell-you that-we-are-the* makers *of-the* famous Double Strength Brakes. These brakes *are believed,* by-*all who* use *them, to-be-the most* reliable *and-the* safest *of all-the* makes at-present *on-the* market. *During-the* month *of*-April *we delivered them* by-*the* gross *to* dealers *in-all-the principal* cities.

If-*you would care to*-test *the* brakes, please *call* at *our* showrooms, *to*-permit *a member of-our* sales staff *to-tell-you all* about *them. We-are* certain *that-you*-will-*be* both *surprised and* pleased if-*you give-them a* trial. *Yours*-truly, (111)

Exercise 74

Dear-Sirs, Since *you have* expressed *a* desire *to* know *something of-our* silk blouses *and* dresses, *we*-take-*the-liberty of* inviting *you to* visit *our* offices *and* salesrooms at 65 Worth Street, *in-this*-city. *We-shall-be*-pleased *to* show *you* samples *of-our* styles *for-this* season. *Our* designs avoid *all* extremes *in* styles *without any* loss *of* charm. *Al*ready record sales *are* reported by-*the* jobbers.

We-have sent *our* catalogue *to-you* by-parcel-post *to*day. *You*-will-note-*that* retail dealers *are* supplied at prices *that*-make *a* strong appeal *to-them*. *Yours*-truly,   (102)

Exercise 75

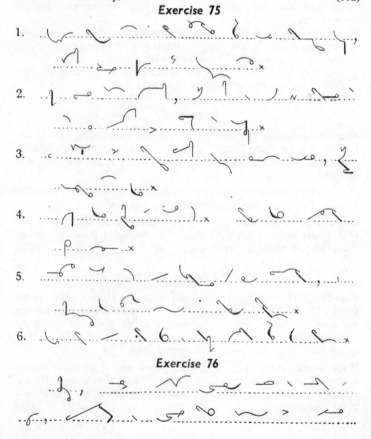

Exercise 76

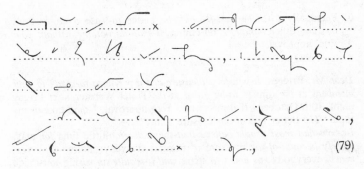

(79)

Exercise 77

1. *I*-am afraid *that-the*-measures *we-have* adopted *are*-not *nearly* strong enough. If-*we*-hope ever *to*-get *Mr.* Crook *to* settle *this* debt, *I-believe it*-will-*be* necessary *to*-bring *more* pressure *to* bear *on him.*

2. *The* property *is* located *on-the* north-west corner *of* Spring Street. *This-is a* good spot *for a* store.

3. *The* price *which-the owners* ask *is remarkably* low; indeed, *the* property *can-be* purchased *to*day *for a* mere trifle *of-its* worth. Originally, *of*-course *the owners* asked *much more for-the building.*

4. *We-are sure that-you*-will *think* favourably *of-this* corner, *and-we*-suggest *that-you* look *it* over *as*-soon-*as*-possible.

5. *It-is near all* transit facilities, *and in-our*-view *you-could*-not locate *your* store *in a more* desirable spot.

6. Manor Park *is a* delightful place *in-the* spring *and* summer. *The* park *is* full *of*-trees, shrubs, *and* flowers.

Exercise 78

1. Please type *an* original *and a* duplicate copy *of-this* lease *for Mr.* Skinner.

2. *I-expect to* fly *to* North Bay *to*morrow, *and-I-shall-be*-glad if-*you*-will meet *me on*-my arrival *to-tell-me everything that-is* necessary about-*the* case.

3. *I-regret that I*-am unable-*to deliver-the* goods *to-you* sooner, *nor is-it* possible *to* say at-present *when*-they *can-be delivered.*

4. *Are-you sure that-the* enclosures were *put in-the* envelope? Yes, *I put them in* personally.

5. Either *we-shall-have to*-take *more* space *in*-some other *building*, or *we-shall-have to*-take *over an* entire floor *in-this building*.

6. Personally *I-believe that-it-would-be* better *to-*lease *a larger* floor *in-*some other *building. Of-*course, *I-shall-do nothing without your* final approval.

Exercise 79

Dear Mr. Bridges, *It-*will-*be a pleasure and a* privilege *to-speak to-your members* at-*the* dinner *to-be given* at-*the* Hotel Webster *next* Friday night, 10th October. If *it* meets *with your* approval, *I-shall* take *as* my topic "*The* Better Use *of-our* Leisure Time."

*I-*know-*that most people believe that-*they-*have too-*little time *for* play, *largely because-of-the* pressure *of* normal everyday affairs. *However, nearly* everybody *has hours to* spare, *and it-is quite surprising how-*much time *is* wasted *because people think* they-*have* no-time *for* leisure. *In-*my *remarks I-shall* endeavour *to* show *that-it-is* worth *an* effort *to-*make *a* better use *of-our* idle *hours. Yours-respectfully,*   (124)

Exercise 80

1. *As we* specialize *in chair* covers, *we-are* able-*to* offer *you* new summer styles at prices *which-are very-*low.
2. *Our* new designs *are very* pleasing *and-*they-*are sure to-*meet *with* favour.
3. *Things which-are* worth *having are* worth working *for. It-is-*not *usually* possible *to* secure *for very-*little or no effort *anything* worth *having.*
4. *It-*will-*be a* privilege *to-*review *this* author's new novel *when-it* appears *next* Thursday. *I-shall-have very-*much *pleasure in* reviewing *it.*
5. *The* fruit crop *was very* big last summer, *largely because-of-the* favourable weather, *and* many farmers *had to-*accept *very-*low-prices.
6. *Our* efforts *to* secure-*the* approval *of-the* bankers were successful. Originally they-were afraid *it-would-*not-*be* possible *to* act favourably *in-our-*case.
7. *The* officials finally decided *to-*make *an* offer *for-the* property *near* River Street.
8. *The special* price at-*which-the* goods *are* offered *is-as* low *as any* ever reached before; *it* scarcely covers-*the* cost *of* freight.
9. *A* circular *which gives-the* new prices *is* enclosed. *You-*will note *that-*they-*are very* reasonable.
10. *There-is a* noticeable decrease *in-our-*business *for-the-*month *of February. Our* Liverpool branch shows *a* drop *of almost* thirty per-cent.

Exercise 81

1. *From all I* gather, *I-believe-that-the* bankers *themselves* favour increasing-*the* average rate *to* three per-cent *and-in* an unofficial manner they endeavoured *to influence the* others *to* adopt *this* course.

2. *The* author, *who had* travelled up-*the* Congo River through darkest Africa, offered *to-speak to-the* gathering *next* Friday night.

3. If only *we* receive-*the* lessons *of* adversity *in a* proper manner, they-*are* likely *to* show us *how to*-lead *a* useful, honourable, *and* successful life.

4. *We-think-you-should*-not *overlook-the* property *being specially* developed by *ourselves near* Riverside Manor. *We should very*-much like *you to* inspect what *we-have to*-offer before-*you* decide *to* buy.

5. *Our* new straws strike *a* fresh note *in* summer styles. *We-think* they-*are-the most* beautiful *we-have* ever offered.

6. *We-believe that-we-had more* business through *our* policy *of* selling at low-prices. *From this you*-will-see *that-it-is* essential *to*-supply these items *for as* little *as*-possible.

7. *We-think-that-the* figures *you-give in-this* estimate *are* incorrect. Either *there-is an* error *in-your* figures, or *you-are* using-*the* wrong grade *of*-leather.

8. *Our* enormous stocks *have to-be* moved *to*-make room *for next* season's goods.

9. *I-think-you-should* reflect *carefully* before-*you* decide *to*-accept *their* offer. They *expect a* reply *from-you* by *next* Thursday.

Exercise 82

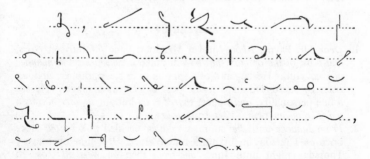

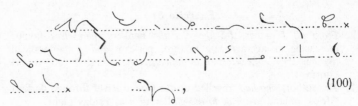

(100)

Exercise 83

1. *Dear*-Sirs, *I-believe-that-the* addressing machine shown *on* page 22 *of-your* monthly bulletin *would-be* suitable *for*-my use, *and*-if *it-is satisfactory*, *I*-may purchase one. *I should-be*-glad if-*you would-have* one-*of-your* salesmen *call* at-my office *to-tell-me more* about-*the* machine.
Please ask-*him to*-'phone before he *comes*, so-*that I*-may-*be* ready *for-him*. *Yours*-truly, (72)
2. *There-is a* train *which* leaves Euston *for* Liverpool at seven o'clock, *and* also *a* train *which* leaves at nine o'clock. *You-can* buy *a* return ticket *for* 10s. (30)
3. Vast changes *have* taken place *in* business *and*-industry *in-the* last ten *years*. *I-believe-that*, *generally*, *the* changes *have-been for-the* better.
4. *There-is*-no-doubt *that* wages *are* higher *and-that*, *in general*, *people* work fewer *hours* than formerly. *However*, *it-is* certainly true *that* workers *have to* specialize *in*-one line *more*-than ever before.
5. *I-have* gone *over-the* records, *and*-*I*-note-*that although-the* business *we-have*-done *with* some firms *has-been* smaller-than *we* hoped, *the* total sales *have-been* better-than *we expected*.

Exercise 84

1. *Dear Mr*. Payne, *I-have*-known *Mr*. John Lane *for* thirteen *years*, *and*-*I*-am *of-the opinion that-he*-will make *a very* desirable *member of-your* club. He began work *with*-us *as a* stenographer, *and*-*has* risen by successive steps *to-the* post *of general* manager. He-*has a* fine personality, *and*-*we*-feel *that-it-is* an honour *to-have-him* as *a member of-our* firm. *Very*-truly-*yours*, (74)
2. *From January* until *the* summer *we-have* decided *to*-keep *our* store open *on*-Thursday nights until nine o'clock. *It*-will-*be* open every Thursday night until June, *and-from* then *on we-shall* close at 5.30 p.m. *as-usual*. (41)

3. *Within-the* past few *years, the* volume *of* business *in-the southern* districts *has-been* much *larger. In*-some industries, business *has-been* better-than *in* similar industries *in-the northern and* eastern districts.

(34)

4. Such industries *as* cotton textiles *have* shown *a* marked increase *in-the* past ten *years. In*-my-*opinion, in-the next* ten *years* there-will-be increases *larger*-than *those that-have-been al*ready noted.   (35)

5. *Because-of-the* lack *of*-rain *in*-some *of-the* western districts *of-*Canada, dust storms *have* often occurred. These storms *have-done* much damage *to* farms *and*-crops.   (29)

6. Some *of-the* districts *in-the* western corn belt *have-been* affected. *Large-numbers of* farms *have-been* covered *in* dust *and it-has-*not-been possible *to*-grow *anything. In*-many-cases, houses *have-been* entirely buried beneath *a* load *of* dust.   (43)

Exercise 85

1. *I-am-*going out-*of* town *next* week, *and-I should* like *to*-talk *with-you* for half *an hour* before *I*-leave. If-*you* happen *to-be in* town *this* week, please *call*-upon me.

2. *I-shall-be in* town *next* Thursday *and-I-shall-be-*glad *to-call-*upon *you* at three o'clock. *I*-am-enclosing *a* rough outline *of what I* propose *to-do for a more* active sales drive *in-the* autumn.

3. Please read *this over* between now *and next* Thursday. If-*you*-will make *a* brief note *in-the*-margin *of anything that* occurs *to-you* we-*can* talk about *it when-we* meet.

4. *Dear-*Sir, *We-have-pleasure in*-enclosing *a* price-list *and* circular which fully describes *our* "Milton Flier."
We-believe-that this machine *is-the most* attractive *and* reliable *we-have* ever offered. *The* machine *of-which-you* speak *is a* foreign one, *and our-own* machine costs *you* only one half *as-much.*
Our local *representative is very* often *in* Cardiff, *and-we-shall* ask-*him to-call-*upon *you and* explain *more* fully *the advantage of owning our* machine. *We*-enclose also *a* list *of-the people in* Cardiff *who-have* bought *this* machine.   (96)

Exercise 86

Dear Miss Brown, *On-your behalf I-have* spoken *to a number-of* persons *in-the* vicinity *of* Woburn Park *with respect to-your* plots. They *all* agreed *that building is-*not *very* active at-*this*-time, *and-I-think there-is-*no-doubt *that,* if-*you* sold-*the* plots *to*day, *you would-*not get *more-*than *you* paid *for-them.*

*A representative of-*one-*of-the* local *building* firms said *that-he believed it-would-be* better *to put them on-the* market *in-the* spring. If-*you* approve, *I-*will ask-*him to put-the* plots *on-his* list *for* sale at not less than £500 each. *This* figure *would-be a* little above-*the* price *you* paid, *and-I-think-that,* even *in-the* spring, *this-is-the most* attractive offer *you-can expect to-*get.

The firm *which this* man *represents is* one-*of-the* best known locally, *and-I-*am-*sure* they-will serve *you to-the* best *advantage. Their* name *and* address *is* Burn & Green, 69 Woburn Park Drive, Brighton.

I-think they-*are-the larg*est *of-the* firms *which-have* built houses *in* Woburn Park. *Their representative* says *that-*they-*have several* plots *of-their-own which* they *expect to-*sell *in-the* spring. *Inasmuch-as you-are* out-*of* town, *I-think it-would-be to-your advantage to-have them* act *on-your behalf. Yours very-*truly, (235)

Exercise 87

1. *Gentlemen,* Recently *I-*bought *a* book *in-your* book department *as a* gift *for a* friend *of-*mine. *I-*found, *however, when I* gave *it to him that-he al*ready *has a* copy *of-this* volume. If-*you do-*not mind, *I-*will return *it and* select *a different* book *of equal* value. *Yours-*truly, (55)

2. *Gentlemen,* Please supply us *with* thirty barrels *of-the* same kind *of* Portland Cement *that-you* supplied *to-*us *on-the third of-*June, at-*the usual trade* terms. *We-*want *this* shipment *delivered to-our-own* pier, *No.* 92. *Yours very-*truly, (45)

3. *Our* magazine *has-been* successful *to an* extent *beyond our* best hopes. *It-is-*now *in-its third year. In-the* second *year we more-*than doubled *the number-of* readers, *and-*now *in-its third year we-*hope *to* treble-*the number.* Every month *it-has-been* necessary *to-*print *more* copies than-*the* month before. *With-the* current issue *we-have* achieved *a* new high mark. *You-*will note-*that-the* magazine *is* bigger *and* better-than ever, *and-the number-of* readers *is larger-*than ever. (89)

Exercise 88

1. *A* man *who wished to-*employ *a* safe driver asked each applicant *how near* he *could* drive *a* car *to-the* edge *of a* cliff. One said *a* foot; *a* second said six-inches. *The third* did-not know. He *had-*not *tried.* He got-*the* job. (47)

2. *Gentlemen, You-*will-see *from-the* enclosed statement *of-your-*account *that* settlement *is very-*much *over*due. *When-the* shipment *was sent to-you,* you *told-*us *that-you would-*make payment *within-the*

usual thirty days—*in*-fact, *you* stated *when-we* opened-*the* account *with-you that-you* planned *to*-take *advantage of-the* cash discount *generally* allowed *for* payment *within* ten days. *You have*-not observed-*the* terms *of-your* agreement, *and-we*-feel *that-we-have* deserved better treatment. *We*-must point-out *that-we-cannot* run *a* successful business unless *the generally* accepted rules regarding credit *are* observed. *We*-want *to*-treat *you* fairly, *but-we-can* not extend-*the* time *for* payment *more*-than *we-have al*ready. *We*-must ask-*you to*-accept-*the* draft *for-the* full amount due *which-we-have* drawn *on-you* through *your* bank *to*day. *Very*-truly-*yours*, (148)

Exercise 89

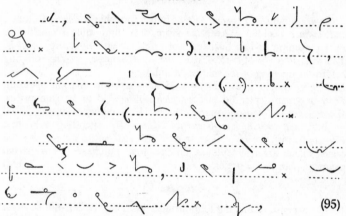

(95)

Exercise 90

1. *Gentlemen*, Kindly let-*me-have your*-price *for* printing *a* hundred copies *of-the* enclosed circular. *I should* prefer *a* better grade *of* paper provided *the* cost *is*-not *too* high. *I should-be*-glad if-*you would* telephone *your*-price *to*-us *as-we-are* in *a* hurry. *Yours very*-truly, (52)

2. *Gentlemen*, *We-are*-sorry *to*-learn *that* two *of-the* books *we* recently *sent to-you* were faulty. Apparently they-were either printed or bound incorrectly. If-*you*-will kindly return *them to*-us, *we-can* obtain credit *for-them ourselves*. *In-the*-meantime, *we-are* mailing-*you* our credit memorandum *for-the* cost *of-the* books plus *the* cost *of*-mailing *them to*-us. *Very*-truly-*yours*, (68)

Exercise 91

Stenography *is a* one hundred per-cent *subject.* By-*that I*-mean *that-you*-must achieve perfect accuracy if-*you-are to-be of* use *in a* business office. *You*-must-*remember that a* business man does-not want *a* typist *who-can* type *his* correspondence *with* only *a* few errors. *You*-must-*be* able-*to give him* only perfect work, perfectly typed *and* properly arranged.

If-*you* wish *to*-make-*sure that-you*-will advance *in-your* business career, *you-should* strive *to* develop-*the* habit *of* accuracy *from-the* beginning *of-your* training. (95)

Exercise 92

We-are planning *a special* sale *of* house furnishings *during* October, *and-we-have* decided *to*-keep-*the* store open until nine o'clock *next* Friday evening so-*that* husband *and*-wife may visit-*the* store *together.* *You*-will *thus* be-able-*to inspect-the* merchandise *we-are* offering before-*the* opening *of-the* sale *on*-Monday.

Everything in-this sale *is be*ing sold at *a very*-low margin *of*-profit. *There-are* many splendid pieces *which*-will-*be* sold at bargain prices. *We-are-sure you*-will-find many articles *which-you* have *al*ways wanted *to* buy, *but which have-been too dear.* By spending *very*-little *you-can* furnish *several* rooms or refurnish *your* entire house. *We-can* easily make arrangements *to* finance *your* purchases *on a* partial payment plan if-*you* prefer. (134)

Exercise 93

1. *The* expense *of*-making long-distance telephone *calls is*-not so *great in-the* late evening. Night messages may also-*be sent* by telegraph at reduced rates.

2. Steps *should-be* taken *to* profit by-*the* statement *of*-accounts just furnished by-*our* auditor.

3. *It-has-been*-found necessary *to*-reduce expenses *in-our* plant, *and it-is* clear *that-we-shall-have* to-*be more* strict *in-our* demands if *a more* favourable *balance is-to-be* shown.

4. If-*you-can come to* town before-*the first of-the*-month, *anything you have to* say relating *to-the* new arrangements *can-be* discussed *with-the* officials *responsible for* making loans.

5. *Gold is* sometimes shipped *from a* country *to-balance that* country's foreign accounts.

6. *Great care is* taken *to guard* these shipments. *When-the* ship reaches dock, *the* bars *of-gold are* shipped at-once *to-the* vault *of a* bank.

7. *Those responsible for-the* shipment take no chances, *and-the gold is* guarded *from-the* moment *it* leaves-*the* ship.
8. *Your* wife *and* children took-*the* noon train *to-the* country, *and-*they-will return about seven o'clock *this* evening.

Exercise 94

1. *Your* note about-*the* German bonds *has-been* referred by-*the* president *to-our* foreign department.
2. Broken by-*the* violence *of-the* wind *and-the* pounding *of-the* waves, *the* vessel ran aground off Point Pleasant.
3. *The* engines *of-the* airplane roared, *the* machine moved up-*the* runway, left-*the* ground, circled three-times above-*the* crowd, *and-*then began *its* flight *to* France.
4. *The* fire engines responded *to-the* sudden summons, *but-*they-were *too-*late *to-*prevent-*the* flames mounting *to-the* top floor.
5. By *a special* arrangement *with-the* hospital departments, many *young* children between-*the* ages *of* four *and* eleven went *to-the* country last-*year.*
6. Some *of-them* travelled by bus, *and* others were *sent* by train. *Those-who-*were *responsible for-the care of-*these children *had a very difficult* task, *but there-*were no accidents *and everything* went splendidly.
7. *Owing to-the* expense *of-the* journey, *large-numbers who* deserved *to-*go were disappointed *and* remained *in* town *all-the* summer.
8. Through-*the* kind assistance *of-several* men *and* women *who-*gave *large* amounts *to-the* funds, *it-was* possible *to* provide extra relief. *We-are* making plans *to-have more* children spend *a* month *in-the* country *next* summer.

Exercise 95

Dear Mr. Freeman, *I-have* recently examined *the* accounts *of-your* department, *and-I-*find *several* expensive items *with nothing to* show *why-the* amounts *have-been* spent. *I-think it-would-be* advisable *to-*make *a special* reference against *any-*such items, *so-that-the* reasons *for-the* payments *would-be* perfectly clear. *I-*don't want *to-be* unduly critical, or unreasonable *in-*my demands, *but your* branch *has* shown disappointing returns *this* year, *and, as you* know, *it-is-*necessary *to-*preserve *a* proper *balance* between expenses *and* earnings.

We agreed last April *to-*discuss *any* un*usual* expenses before they-were incurred, *and-I-*must ask-*you to* observe *our* agreement. *Very-*truly-*yours,*

(116)

Exercise 96

Gentlemen, We-have-been out-*of* touch *with your* firm *for*-some-time through no fault *of-our-own.* Permit us *to*-suggest *that-it-would-be* advisable *and* certainly *more* profitable *for-you* if-*your* salesman *would call more* often. *It-is generally* admitted by-*the different* agents *of* rival firms *that-it-is* extremely *difficult to*-keep up-*the* sales *of* cotton print goods unless *something is* done *to*-keep *in* close touch *with-the* buyers. *It-is* known *that your* lines *are as* attractive *as-the* others, *and you ought to-have* no *great-difficulty in* proving *that* fact. *We*-know *that-you*-will regard-*the* hint *we-have* offered *as nothing but* evidence *of-our* kind feelings *for-you. Very*-truly-*yours*, (125)

Exercise 97

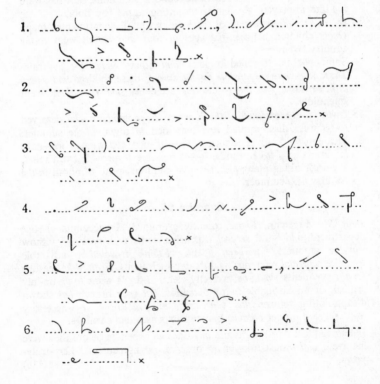

Exercise 98

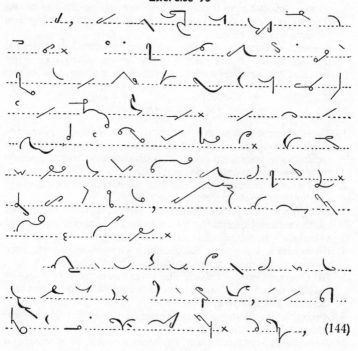

(144)

Exercise 99

1. *Your* attention *is called to-the* fact *that* students must register *for-the* summer session before 4th-July.
2. *In-this* division *we* insist *on a* written final examination *in* every extension course.
3. *Thank-you for-the* explanation *of-the different* items *on-your* statement. *I*-am-enclosing my remittance *in* full payment *of-the* account.
4. *Because-of* business expansion, *it*-will-*be*-necessary *to*-employ *more* people. *It-is our* intention *to* engage only *those-who-have had a* thorough professional training.
5. *In*-some *large* firms, typists work *in a general* correspondence division. Somebody *is usually* appointed *who-is* responsible *for-the* work *of-this* department.

6. *The different members of-the* firm *do-*not-*have their-own* private sec-
   retaries. Instead *a* girl *is* assigned *to-them* by-*the* person *who-has-the*
   supervision *of-the* correspondence division. *This* arrangement
   prevents waste *of-*time.
7. *I-expect to* travel *to* Bristol *to*morrow *to* attend-*the* National
   Business Show. Please reserve *a* seat *for-me* on-*the* train *which*
   leaves at 9.30 a.m. *and* wire *a* reservation *for a* room at-*the* Barnes
   Hotel.

Exercise 100

1. *The* selection *of a* vocation *is-*not *an* easy task. *Generally it-should-be
   to-your advantage to* secure assistance *from* somebody *who*
   specializes *in* vocational counsel. *A* discussion *with-*such *a* person
   should assist *you to-*make-up *your* mind.
2. *Almost without* exception, entrance examinations *for-those-who*
   wish *to-*train *for-the* professions *are difficult.*
3. *Our* gift shop *and* notions section *are two* departments *of-the* store
   which-have some exceptional values just-now. *You-*will-find *it* easy
   *to-*make *a* selection, *for-there-is a* wide choice.
4. If-*you* wish *to* select some books *to-*take *with-you* on-*your* vacation,
   we-have a wide range *of* new fiction *in-our* book section.
5. *The Chair*man said: "*I should* like *to-have an* expression *of opinion
   from-the* floor." *A* motion *to-*go ahead *with-the* transaction *was*
   seconded *and* approved.
6. *A* reception at-*the* station *is-to-be* planned *for-the* flyer *who-has* just
   returned *from* South-America.
7. *To-the* best *of-*my recollection, *there-was-*no intention *of* charging *a*
   registration fee *for-this* course.
8. *In-*anticipation *of* increased sales, *we-are* opening *a* branch *of-our*
   business *in-the southern* section *of-the* city. *We-have* selected *a*
   favourable location, *and-we-believe-that our* chances *are* exception-
   ally bright.

Exercise 101

Dear Mr. Newman, *We-are having a* celebration *on* 14th October
*to-*mark-*the* anniversary *of-the* founding *of-our* college. *On-this*
occasion *there-*will-*be a* dinner, *and-in-*addition *there-*will-*be several*
addresses by *people whose* reputation *is* nation wide.
One-*of-*these talks *is-to-be delivered* by John Goschen, *whose* reputation
as an author *is* second *to* none. *A* presentation *to Mr.* Goschen *has-been*
arranged.

In expectation *that-you*-will *wish to* attend, *I*-am-enclosing *a* ticket. Additional tickets may-*be* obtained *from-the* secretary upon application. *We-are* restricting invitations *to* past *and*-present students. *Yours-respectfully,*

(107)

Exercise 102

Dear-Sir, *To* secure *a* wider distribution *of-our* book "Educational Occupations *for* Children," *we-are* making, *for-this* month only, *quite a* reduction *in-the*-price. *As a special* attraction *we-have* issued *a* presentation edition *in* leather *which* sells *for* only one guinea. Bound *in* imitation leather, *the* book costs 17s. 6d.

The book *would-be a very* valuable addition *to-your* library. *It gives* full directions *for*-many educational occupations *for* children *of all* ages, *and,* through-*the* use *of* excellent illustrations, *all-the* directions *are very*-simple.

If-you-like, *we-can* dispatch-*the* book *to-you for-your* approval, *and*-if-*you* decide *to*-return *it,* *you*-may *do*-so *without any* obligation. *Very*-truly-*yours,*

(123)

Exercise 103

1. Please *call Mr.* Nation *on-the* telephone, *and tell-him that-the* illustrations *are near*ly ready. Mention *that*-they-will-*be delivered to*morrow.

2. *The* addition *to-the* nation's population *during-the* year exceeded *any* increase *in* former *years.*

3. Many *of-the people in-the organization believe-that-the* situation *is* so bad *that-the* opposition faces defeat *in-the* national election.

4. *Doctor* Foster *remarked*: "By-*all*-means take *a* vacation, *and* exercise caution *to*-avoid *any-more colds.*"

5. *Dear*-Sir, *We-are*-pleased *to inform-you* that *your* application *for* admission *to-the* College *of* Physicians *and* Surgeons *has-been* accepted. *Your* references *have-been* carefully examined, *and-the*-result *of-our investigation has-been* entirely *to-our satisfaction. We*-may say *that-the information* now *in-our* possession reflects *very*-much *to-your* credit. *Very*-truly-*yours,*

(60)

Exercise 104

Dear Doctor Brown, *I-wish to*-make application *for-the* position *of* secretary, details *of-which* appear *in to*day's "Tribune."

I-am 21 *years of*-age. *I*-received *a* good business education, *and* obtained *an* honours diploma *in* stenography.

For-the past *two-years I-have* acted *as* secretary *to Doctor* Brewster, *who-is, I-think,* known *to-you. During this*-time *I-have* carried out-*the* usual office duties, *and, in*-addition, *I-have-taken-the doctor's special* dictation. *I*-know-*that* my employer *is* satisfied *with* my services. *I should* like, *however, to* secure *a* position *in*-my-own town.

Doctor Brewster *has* kindly *given me* permission *to-refer-you to-him for-any information* regarding my ability. If-*you wish me to-tell-you anything-more to* assist *you in* making *a* decision *I-shall-be*-glad *to do*-so. *Yours*-truly, (145)

Exercise 105

Gentlemen, Your representative called on-us *yesterday, and* gave us full *information* regarding *your publications. We*-were-not able *yesterday to*-make *a* final decision, *but* upon reflection *we*-feel *that-we-can* display *to advantage* certain *of-the* titles *in-your* catalogue.

Please *deliver to*-us at-once *a* dozen copies each *of*

        A Dictionary *of* Education;
        Public Finance;
        Corporation Law.

If-*you have*-no *objection, we-shall* return *any of*-these books *which-we*-find *do*-not sell readily.

Please keep-us *informed of any* new books *which-are published* by-*your organization. Very*-truly-*yours,* (98)

Exercise 106

Gentlemen, Because-of-our decision *to* erect *a building of-our-own, we-shall*-not-*be in a* position *to*-renew *our* lease *when-it* expires *next year*. Permit us *to*-take *this* occasion *to-thank-you for-the*-many courtesies *you have al*ways extended *to*-us.

Preparations *for-the* erection *of-our* new offices *and* salesrooms *are go*ing ahead nicely, *but-there-is* just *a* chance *that our* new *building* may-not-*be* ready before-*the* expiration *of-our* lease. *We wish to*-make provision *for-any* un*expected* delays, *and*-if-*you do*-not object, *we should* like *to-have your* permission *to*-remain *in-this* building, if-necessary, *for* not-*more*-than three-months, at-*the* present rental. *We*-hope-*you*-will-*have* no *objection to-this* arrangement. *Very*-truly-*yours,* (133)

Exercise 107

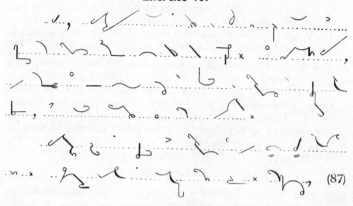

(87)

Exercise 108

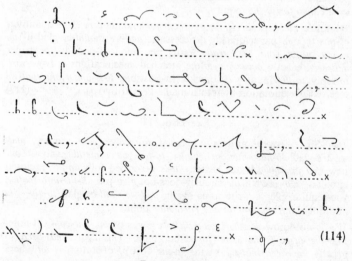

(114)

Exercise 109

1. *The* bearer *of-this*-note, *Mr.* James White, *is a* close personal friend *of*-mine. He-*is* travelling *to* Canada, *and* he-will-*be in* Glasgow *for a* few days before sailing.

I-want *Mr.* White *to*-meet *you, for I*-know-*that-you*-will-*be*-glad *to number him* among *your* acquaintances. *For-this*-reason *I-do*-not-feel *that I*-am imposing *on-your*-kindness *in* asking-*you to* show *Mr.* White some *of-the important* sights *of-the* city. *I-think-that-you* and he *should* find *your*selves fully *in accord on-most subjects.* (98)

2. *You have always-been in* sympathy *with our child* training campaign by-*which we* try *to put as* many children *as*-possible *in* camp *for a* few weeks each summer. *Our* campaign *has*-now started again, *and-we*-enclose *a* book *of* seals. These stamps cost *you* only 3s. 6d. *As you* know, these children *are cared for* by councillors *who-give their* services free, *and* every penny collected *in-our* campaign *is* spent *on-the* children. (79)

Exercise 110

Gentlemen, We-have received *a* request *for a* quotation *on a large* quantity *of* news-print paper, *but it-is impossible for*-us *to* supply-*the* paper *from our-own* mills *because-we-cannot* make-*it* up *on* rollers *as-is called for in-the* inquiry.

We-know-*that-you have-the* equipment *for*-making *very large* quantities *of-this* type *of* paper quickly if-necessary, *and-we should-be*-glad if-*you* would quote *your* best *trade* terms per hundred-pounds *for* paper *delivered* exactly *according-to-the* attached specifications. *As-we-wish to*-reply *to-the* inquiry *as* quickly *as*-possible, *it-is-important that-we* receive *your* quotation by-return-mail. *Very*-truly-*yours,* (117)

Exercise 111

Dear-Sir, *We*-were *especially* pleased *to*-receive *your* inquiry, *and-we-are*-glad *to-have-the* opportunity *to-tell-you something* about *our* new *and improved* water heater. *It-is* described fully *in-the* enclosed circular. *However,* if-*the* circular does-not *give-you all-the information you*-require, please write *to*-us again, *and-we-shall-be*-glad *to-give-you* additional *information on any particular* points.

We-do-not-know *whether you* wish *to* use gas or oil, *but-you*-will-note-*that-the* price *is-the* same *for* either type. *This* heater *has-been* so *greatly improved that-the* saving *in-the* cost *of* operation *is any*where *from a* quarter *to a* half *of-the* former cost.

These heaters *are*-now *on* display by dealers everywhere throughout-*the* country, *and-we*-suggest *that-you* inspect them at-*the* first *opportunity. Your* local dealer *would-be*-glad *to-tell-you which* heater *would-be* adequate *for-your* requirements, *for-it-is-important to-have-the* right size. He-*would-be*-glad *to-give-you* also *particulars of-the* cost *of* installation.

We-have returned-*the* stamps *which-you* enclosed *with your* inquiry. *Very*-truly-*yours*, (198)

Exercise 112

1. Will-*you* kindly let-*me*-know where *I*-might obtain *a* copy *of-the* book *published* some-time-ago *which* embodied *the* results *of an investigation* by *several* scholars into-*the importance of* physical training. *I-cannot* find *it any*where. (40)
2. *I-shall* catch-*the* three o'clock train *from* town. Will-*you* be-able-*to* meet *me* at-*the* station? *I should-be* unwilling *to*-impose *on-your*-kindness, *and-I-do*-not-know *whether you*-will-*be* free *to*-meet *me*. If my request *is an* imposition, please ignore *it*. (50)
3. While *I-was* delighted *to*-learn *how* well *the* scholars did *in-the* history examination, *I-was*-not *greatly surprised in*-view *of-the great care with-which their* preparation *was* planned. (32)
4. While *I*-am *quite* willing *to-believe that-this* method *of* shipment *is an improvement, and-that-there-would-be an important* saving, *I-think-we should* wait until *we-have-had an opportunity to-tell whether it*-will-*be* satisfactory. Meanwhile, *I-think-the larg*est portion *of-our* shipments *should go according-to-the usual* method. (57)

Exercise 113

1. Habits may-*be* good or bad, helpful or harmful.
2. *We-think it-would-be* fairer if *all* helped *the* Neighbourhood Workers' Club *according-to* their means. Everyone *cannot give an equal* amount. Some *people could give more*-than others.
3. Perhaps *this particular opportunity* may not occur again, *and-we-shall-be* greatly *surprised* if-*you* don't hasten *to*-accept.
4. *The gentleman to* whom *the* house *was* leased *was quite surprised to*-receive *a* request *for* higher rent.
5. *In-the* Wall Street district *of*-Manhattan *the great* height *of-the buildings* makes-*the* streets seem smaller-*than* they actually *are*. *On*-Sundays *and* holidays, *when-the* streets *are* deserted, *the buildings are* even *more* imposing—they take *on-the* appearance *of* tall cliffs. (45)
6. *The* good secretary does-not *al*ways *have* her hat *on* in readiness *to*-leave-*the* office at five o'clock. *There-are* times *when important*

correspondence must *be* answered, *and* she *should* show her loyalty *to-*her employer *and* help *him* by not leaving-*the* office until *the* replies *are in-the* post. She *should* hold herself *in* readiness *for-*these occasions. *In-the* average office they-*do-*not occur often.

(70)

Exercise 114

Gentlemen, We wish to acquire *several* pieces *of-*land *in* Hamilton *near-the* property *we-*now hold, *for-the* purpose *of* housing-*the* whole *of-our* assembling work *in a* new plant *which-we* propose *to* erect. Perhaps *you-*will *tell-*us promptly if-*you* hear *of any* land *to-be* offered *for* sale, *and-thus give-*us *an opportunity to* investigate.

We-are anxious *to* begin work *on-our* new plant *this* autumn. If-*we-do-*not purchase *the* land *within-the* next *two-*months, *there-is* every likelihood *that-we-shall-have to* postpone operations until *the* spring. *Any information you-*may obtain *for-*us will-*be a very great* help. *Very-*truly-*yours,* (118)

Exercise 115

*Dear-*Sir, *When-you* hang up *your* hat *and* begin *to* answer *the* pile *of-*correspondence awaiting-*you on-your* desk, *have-you* ever thought *of what* happens *when your* mail *is* received by-*the* person *to* whom *it-is* addressed? *Remember-that-the first* impression *your* correspondent receives *is from-the* notepaper he holds *in-his* fingers.

Most business men *believe in-the* value *of* appearances, *and* pay *great* attention *to most things which* place *their* firm high *in-the* estimation *of-their* correspondents, *but it-is surpri*sing how-many *quite over*look-*the opportunity* paper offers *of* expressing-*the* standing *of-their* firm.

*We-*hope-*you-*will exercise *care with-this particular* detail. Perhaps *you-*will permit us *to-*quote *for* quantity lots *on-our* "Distinctive Bond" *according-to your-*requirements. *Very-*truly-*yours,* (135)

Exercise 116

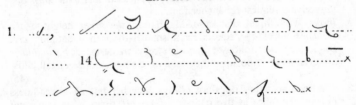

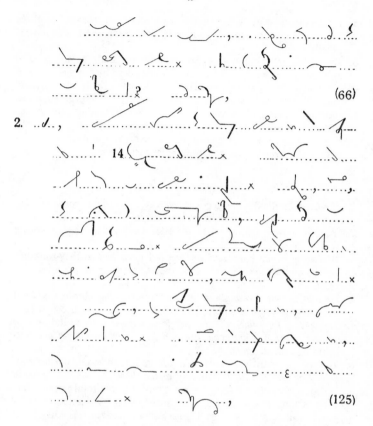

(66)

(125)

Exercise 117

1. *The* house *is* equipped *with* standard fixtures, *and* every need *in a* modern home *is* filled.
2. *The* attached card, *when* filled *in and* mailed, will-bring-*you a* detailed statement *of-the*-cost *of-this* heater installed *in-your* home.
3. Merchandise bought *from-the* middle *to-the* end *of-the*-month will-*be* billed *to-you in February*.
4. These bonds *are* sound, *and* at-*the* current prices *you*-will-*be* assured *of a satisfactory* yield.

5. *I* telephoned *your* office *to*day, *and told-them that-we* need-*the* thousand posters quickly. Please send-*them to-*us *as*-soon-*as*-possible.

6. *Dear*-Madam, Undoubtedly *your child* or children will need *a number-of* play-suits *this* summer. *The* suits described *in-the* enclosed circular *are most* attractive. They-*are* designed *for* hard wear, *and* you-will-note *that-the*-prices *are quite* reasonable. *The* prices *are* so moderate *that-you-can* afford *to* buy *two* instead-*of* one at-*the* ordinary prices. They-*are* made up *in* sizes *for* children *two to* ten *years* old. Just indicate *on-the* form *how*-many *you* need, *and*-they-will-*be delivered to-you* promptly. *Very*-truly-*yours*, (95)

Exercise 118

1. *We-have* credited *your*-account *with-the* thousand *yards of* felt *that-you do*-not need *and-have sent* back *to*-us.

2. *You*-will-not-*be*-able-*to* select *a* better territory *in-which to*-locate *your* factory.

3. *We* wrote *to-the* bank *and-we* received *word that as*-they-were-not able-*to* collect-*the* second note they-*had*-not *tried to* collect-*the third*.

4. *He told*-us *that-he-would* send-us *a* remittance, *but-that-he could*-not undertake *to* pay-*the* whole debt while *trade was* so uncertain.

5. *Thank-you for-your* promptness *in*-sending-*the* thousand-feet *of* copper wire. *We-are*-enclosing *our* cheque *which* covers *our* outstanding indebtedness.

6. *The* last shipment *was short* by *a* hundred-pounds, *and our* account *should-be* credited *for-the*-amount *of-the short*age.

7. Will-*you* please try *to*-find *for-me a* report *of-the* total imports *and* exports through-*the* Port *of* Vancouver *during-the* last-*year*.

8. *The* belt illustrated *on* page 4 *is very* smart, *and it-is-the* sort-*of* belt *which-would* look well *with a* sports outfit.

Exercise 119

1. *It-is* often felt *that a* speed *of* 80 *words a* minute *in shorthand is* adequate *for* ordinary business purposes. *However*, some employers require *a* higher degree *of* skill, *and*-they-will-not employ *a* stenographer *who-cannot* write 120 *words a* minute. (43)

2. *When-you* leave *school, with a certificate which* states *that-you have* passed *a* test dictated at perhaps 80 *words a* minute, *you*-must-*remember that-you-are*-not fully equipped *to*-meet every demand

of-the business world, *and you-should* endeavour *to improve your* skill *and your knowledge.* If-*you wish to* secure *a* position *which* pays *a* good salary, *you-should* acquire *a* speed *of* at-least *a* hundred-*words a* minute *on all* types *of* dictation. (80)

Exercise 120

1. Perhaps-*the most important* asset *of a* good stenographer *is a* sound *knowledge-of* words. *You-should* know-*the* meanings *of as* many words *as*-possible *as*-well-*as-the shorthand* outlines *for-them. This-is your* stock *in trade,* so *to-speak.* (43)
2. *An* excellent method *of* increasing *your knowledge-of* words *and your shorthand* skill *is to*-write articles dictated *from a* newspaper or magazine. If-*you do*-not-know-*the* meanings *of*-some *of-the words,* look *them* up *in a* dictionary *immediately.* If-*you-cannot do-this* at-once, place *a* circle around these *words, and*-find out *their* meanings *when an opportunity* presents *itself.* (65)
3. *A very*-good way *to* increase *your knowledge-of shorthand* outlines *is to*-read plenty *of*-literature written *in shorthand. Always-be sure to*-look up-*the* meanings *of any words you do*-not-*under*stand. (35)

Exercise 121

Dear Mr. Wilson, *I*-fear *that-it*-will-not-*be* possible *for-me to* attend-*the* discussion *next* Thursday night. *I-have*-just received *word that I*-must make *a* trip out-*of*-town, *and-I-do*-not *expect to*-return before Friday. *However,* if-*it-is*-possible *for-me to* attend *I-shall* certainly *do*-so, *for I-wish to* show my support *of-your* plans.

I-am sending my cheque *for* five-pounds *which-is to-be* applied *towards-the building* fund. *You*-will *under*stand-*the spirit in-which-it-is sent, and* my name need-not-*be* mentioned *when-you acknowledge-the* gift. *Very*-truly-*yours,* (110)

Exercise 122

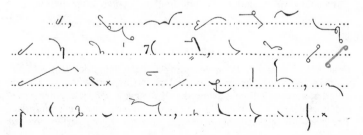

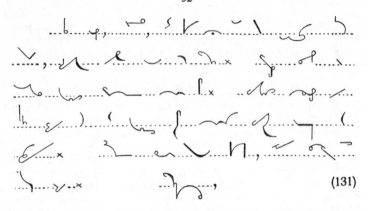

(131)

Exercise 123

1. *We-have*-not heard *from-you* regarding *your*-order *for* calenders. About *a* month ago *we-sent-you* a folder *which* illustrated *the* attractive designs *we-have* prepared *for-the* Christmas *trade*. *It-would-be* well *to*-place *your*-order *as*-early-*as*-possible *to*-make sure *that-the* calendars will-*be delivered in*-time.

   Perhaps *this year you would* like *to* substitute *a* small bill holder. *We-can* supply *them in* imitation leather *in* gross lots at *very* moderate prices. (81)

2. *Thank-you for-your*-letter *of yesterday*. *We-are*-glad *to*-receive *your* reminder *that our* order *for* calenders *should-be* in-hand.

   Will-*you* please send-us further *particulars of-the* bill holders? *We*-may-make *a* change *this year*, *and* distribute *them* instead-*of-the* calendars. If-*you*-will attend *to-this* matter *immediately*, *we*-will send *our* order by-return-mail. *We-are* afraid *that-we-are* later *this year in* placing *our* order, *but-we-are-sure that-we*-may rely upon receiving-*the* calendars or bill holders by-*the* latter part *of-this* month. (98)

Exercise 124

Dear Mr. Alexander, *We-are*-sending-*you this* reminder *that on and*-after 1*st February* the price *of-the* Porter Car, *with-the* new sixteen cylinder motor, will-*be* advanced. *We*-suggest *that-you* enter *your*-order *immediately*, so-*that-you*-may secure *your* car at-*the* current price. *You* need-not take *delivery of-the* car at-once. If-*you* prefer, *you-can* place *your*-order now, at-*the* present price, *and you*-may take *delivery of-the* car *several* months later.

We-do-not-*think-you*-will ever *have* another *opportunity of* buying one-*of*-these beautiful cars at-*the* current price, *and-we*-suggest *that-you* permit *our representative to-call and*-interview *you* about-*the* matter. *We*-enclose *a* stamped addressed envelope *for-your*-reply. *Very*-truly-*yours*, (132)

Exercise 125

1. *We-think-there-is* no-longer *any*-doubt *that within-the next* few *years the* motion picture industry will *undergo a* marked change.

2. *We-are-informed that-the* natural gas industry *has a wonderful* future.

3. Please-*do*-not ship-*the* remainder *of-our* order until *the* latter part *of*-September.

4. *We-can* send-*you information of a general* nature only. If-*you* need further *particulars, therefore, it-would-be* better *to* arrange *for-an* interview *with-the writer of-this*-letter.

5. *Our* sales increased *in November and* December, *and-we*-hope *that-the improvement* will-*be* maintained *for-the* remainder *of-the* winter.

6. Educators *in-the* past few *years have*-taken *great-interest in-the* development *of-character, for-it-is believed that-the* nation's future depends upon-*the character of-its* citizens *rather*-than upon-*their knowledge.*

7. *I*-am *interest*ed *in-your* refrigerator. Will-*you* kindly send *a* full *description of-it, as*-well-*as-the* total cost installed *in*-my home. *I-wish to* install *a* refrigerator not-later-than *the* end *of-this* week, so *I-shall-be*-obliged if-*you*-will let-*me-have this information* promptly upon receipt *of-this*-letter. (58)

8. *The* invention *of-the* typewriter rendered *shorthand a very* valuable art. *In*-order-*to* meet-*the* demands *of-the* business world, *it-is*-necessary *to-be an* accurate *shorthand writer and a* skilful operator *of-the* typewriter. *The two subjects are* sometimes *called-the* twin arts.

The object of-your shorthand training *is to* enable-*you to*-take dictation so-*that-you*-may write-*the* matter dictated rapidly. *In*-order-*that-you*-may acquire *a* high degree *of* skill *in* writing *from-your shorthand*-notes, *you-should* typewrite *the* letters or-other-matter dictated *in-your* lessons *as* often *as you* possibly *can.* (103)

Exercise 126

Within-the last few *years the number-of* motor scooters making-*their-*way along-*the* roads *of-our* country *has-been* rapidly increasing, *and-we-think-there-is very-*little doubt *that-this* method *of-*travel *has a great* future. *The* motor scooter *has in-*many-cases replaced *the* bicycle *of* earlier days, *because-it-is* swifter *and* smarter. *It-has* many supporters, *especially in-the* remoter districts *which-are* out-*of-the* way *of-the* railways, where *it represents a* means *of-*bringing *people* into closer touch *with-the large* centres.

Because-of-the small size *of-the* motor scooter *which* renders *it* easy *to-*manage *on* narrow roads many-*people are* favourably disposed *towards it. This* feature *can-be* better *under*stood if-*we* picture *a large* vehicle seeking *to* pass *a* scooter *on a* narrow road.

Those-who object to motor scooters *do-*so *because, in-their-opinion,* motor scooters *are* adding *to-the* amount *of* traffic *al*ready *on-our* roads. *But-the* scooter *is* safer *and* less noisy than-*the* motor cycle, *and-*will, *we-think, be* used by *more and more people in-the* future. (188)

Exercise 127

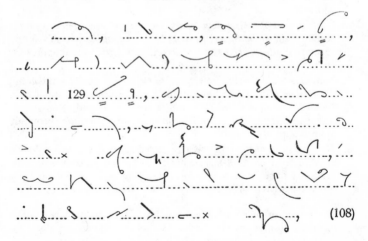

(108)

Exercise 128

1. *Dear Mr.* Taylor, *This*-letter will introduce *to-you Mr.* Robert P. Johnson, *who-is in-your* city *on* business *for-his* company. *His* firm *has under*taken *a* contract *of*-some magnitude *in-the* planning *of a* community centre *for-this*-city, *and* consequently *Mr.* Johnson *is* anxious *to* study at *first hand what-has-been* accomplished *in-your* city.

   I-am confident *that-you*-will-*do all-you-can to*-make *Mr.* Johnson comfortable while he-*is with-you, and-I-shall* consider *all-that-you do for-him a very-great* favour *to-me.* Sincerely *yours,* (98)

2. *Gentlemen, In* response *to-your* communication *of* 14th-September *we-are*-sorry *to* say *that-we-cannot* consider *your*-request *for an* exclusive agency *for-the* sale *of-our* goods *in-your* city. *It-is* contrary *to-our* policy *to*-restrict *the* sale *of-our* merchandise *to any* one wholesale firm *in a* city, *and-for-this*-reason *we-cannot* take-*advantage of-your* offer. *We-are-sure that-you*-will recognize *that, in* fairness *to all-our* dealers, *it-is-impossible to*-make *a* departure *from our* policy.

   If-*you*-will continue *to hand*le *our* goods at-*the usual* wholesale terms, *we-are-sure that-you*-will-*be* completely satisfied *with your* sales. *The* new lines *we-have* recently introduced *have* met *with* considerable favour *all-over-the*-country, *and-we-are* confident *that*-they-will sell *to-your* complete *satisfaction. Very*-truly-*yours,* (145)

Exercise 129

Gentlemen, As a consequence *of-your* inconsistent conduct *in-the*-matter *of-our* contract, *we-are* compelled *in* self-defence *to* state *that* unless *you-can* complete-*the* order *by-the* end *of-the*-month, *the* business must at-once *be* transferred, *as-the* delays *which-have* occurred *have* placed us *in* considerable *difficulties.*

At *our* interview *in*-September, *when-you signified your* willingness *to under*take-*the* contract, *you*-were confident *that-you could deliver* half-*the* goods *by-the* end *of* October *and-the balance* by-*the first of*-December.

These conditions were-not complied *with* so far *as-the first* part-*of-the* agreement *was* concerned, *and, on-our* complaining about-*the* unnecessary delay, *you* stated *that-the* whole *would-be delivered* by December. *It-is*-now *the* 14th, *and-in-the* interval *we-have* communicated *with-you on-several* occasions *without-the* desired result. *We-have come to-the* conclusion *that* future contracts *should-be*-placed *with*-one-*of-your* competitors. *The significance of-this should*-not-*be* lost upon *you, and it*-will-*be to-your advantage to* fulfil *your* obligations *without* further delay. *Yours*-truly, (190)

Exercise 130

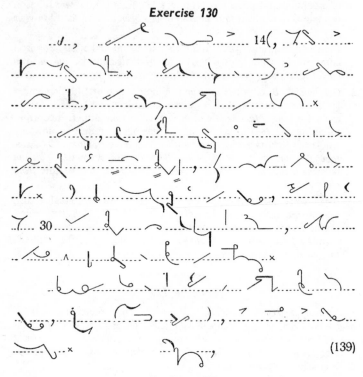

(139)

Exercise 131

1. Will-*you* kindly forward *instructions* concerning-*the* transfer *of-your* stock *certificates.*
2. *Several circumstances* rendered *it impossible to* accomplish *much* at-*the* last meeting *of-the* committee. *We-are therefore* trying *to* secure another hearing.
3. *The* majority *of-the members of-the* committee *are of-the* opinion *that inasmuch-as-the improvement* is still *in-the* experimental stage,

it-should-not-*be* adopted until *it-has-been* tried further. Consequently, *we-think-we-shall-be* compelled *to* content *ourselves with-the publication of a* minority report. (51)

4. Please forward *to*-us one dozen men's sweaters *in* assorted colours, size 36. *We-are* forwarding *to-you to*day six women's woollen scarves. *We* ordered *them on-the under*standing *that-we would-have-the* privilege *of*-returning *them* if-*we*-found *there-was*-not *sufficient* demand *for-them*. *There-is*-no *prospect whatever of* selling *them*, so *there-is*-no reason *for* keeping *them in* stock *any*-longer. (69)

5. *Probably-the* illustrations will-*be* completed *to*morrow morning. Will-*you* please advise us *whether you wish* us *to* charge each illustration *individually*, or *shall we* just send one bill *giv*ing *the* total cost? (34)

Exercise 132

1. *The* rise *in* prices *is governed* by *circumstances beyond our* control. *In-all-probability there*-will-*be a* drop *in* price *when-the* supply *is sufficient to*-meet-*the* demand.

2. *A* report covering *the* export *and* import *trade is* issued annually by-*the Government*, through-*the* Department *of* Commerce.

3. *Most of-the large* department stores *advertise regular*ly *in-the* daily newspapers. *Whenever* they hold *a special* sale, *and particular*ly at Christmas *and* Easter, *when people do more* shopping than *usual, the* stores increase-*the* size *of-their advertisements*. *It-would-be interest*-ing *to* know *whether-the* additional sales *are sufficient to*-cover-*the* expense *of advertis*ing. Evidently *it-is sufficiently* profitable, *for-the* stores continue *their* campaigns *without* interruption. *Probably-the* stores *have a* method *of* estimating fairly accurately *whether* they-*are* getting full value *from-their advertis*ing campaigns.

In-addition *to regular* newspaper *advertis*ing, many *of-the* stores *advertise* by direct mail, *that-is*, they send announcements *to individual* customers *call*ing-*their* attention *to special* offerings. (116)

Exercise 133

The majority *of*-us agree *in-the*-matter *of*-recognizing *and* admitting *that-the cheer*fulness *of* others *has* often *been* instrumental *in* helping *and* comforting us *in* trying *circumstances*. Some *people* seem *to-think-that cheer*fulness *is-the* result *of*-thoughtlessness, *but* fortunately these *individuals are in-the* minority.

To-our way *of-think*ing, *cheerfulness is generally the* result *of-*thought-fulness *and* kindly feelings *of* friendship. Bearing *in* mind *our thank*-fulness *for cheerful and* friendly *words in-*time *of-*trouble, *we should* persistently strive *to-*avoid complaining or whining about hardships.

The popularity *of a cheerful* personality, *and-the* unpopularity *of-those individuals who* carry *with-them an* air *of* hopelessness *and cheer*-lessness, *is instructive. But* apart *from* helping others, *we* benefit *ourselves from a* psychological *and* physiological point *of-*view, *as-it-is a* fact *that* health *can-be improved* through *a* mental attitude *of* optimism *and cheer*fulness. (148)

Exercise 134

(142)

Exercise 135

1. *Dear*-Sir, *We-are*-sending-*you* herewith *a* final notification *that-the* quarterly premium *on-your insurance* policy *number* 42,691 *is* payable *on* 25th-March, *that-is, in two*-days. *Two* previous notices *have-been sent to-you*.

   You-will realize *the danger of*-permitting *the* policy *to* lapse through *neglect*ing *to* pay-*the* premium *in*-time. Serious *financial* loss may-*be-the* result *of*-such *neglect. Very*-truly-*yours*,   (74)

2. *Dear*-Sir, Experience shows *that very* frequently *a* courteous note pointing-out *that an* account *is over*due results *in* prompt settlement.

   No-doubt *you have neglected to* pay *your* bill through *care*lessness, *but-you*-will note *that-the* account really *should-have-been* paid some-time-ago. *We should* appreciate receiving *your* remittance at-*the* earliest possible moment. *Your* co-operation *in-this*-matter will-*be very*-much appreciated. *Very*-truly-*yours*,   (71)

3. *Gentlemen, We-are*-now carrying *a* complete line *of* radios *and* pianos *in-our* furniture department. Many *different* makes *are represented in-the* instruments *we-are* showing, *and you*-will *thus have a* convenient *opportunity of* seeing *and* comparing *the* various makes.

   You-may purchase *any* instrument *you* desire *and you-can* pay *for-it* at-*your* convenience *in* easy instalments. Cordially-*yours*,
                                                                           (63)

4. *Gentlemen, We-sent-you to*day *the* following *telegram:* "Material received *has* wrong finish. *Exchange for* quality specified *in* order." *We-would* appreciate *your* shipping *the* material *of-the* correct quality *and*-finish *immediate*ly. *Yours*-truly,   (35)

5. *Gentlemen, We* frequently *have* inquiries *for* outdoor furniture *in-our* hardware department, *and-we-believe that-it-would-be* worth showing *a* limited variety *of* garden *chairs and* tables, etc. Will-*you* kindly ask *your representative to-call when-he-is in-this* neighbourhood *to-give*-us *a* few suggestions. Sincerely *yours*,   (52)

Exercise 136

You-may-*be interest*ed *in-the* following theory concerning-*the* periodic appearance *of* depression *in almost all*-branches *of-trade*. Experience shows *that-the most-probable* cause *of-this* common trouble *is that* prices-*have* suddenly fallen, after *a* period *of* speculation *during which* prices *have-been* un*usually* high. *The* high-prices occasioned *during-the* period *of* speculation may-*have* resulted *from-the* expectation *of a shortage in-the* supply *of*-some *particular* commodity, or-some-other similar cause. Eager buying helps *to* produce-*the expected* rise *in* prices, *and-the first* buyers seem *to-have-the* ability *to*-make huge profits. *Their* success encourages others, *and-the* speculative *spirit* spreads *to all* commodities. Borrowers use *all-their* credit, bankers *are* willing *to*-lend, *and a general spirit of* recklessness prevails.

After *a* while, *however, the* upward trend *of*-prices ceases. *When-those-who* hold stocks *wish to*-realize, *a* reaction *comes and*-prices begin *to* fall. They start falling so rapidly *that* everyone seems-*to-be* losing. Credit *is* obtained only *with great difficulty*. No-one will part *with* ready-money, or postpone *his* claim *to-it*. Merchants *cannot* meet *their* obligations, *and* many firms fail *because* they-*are* unable-*to* obtain-*the* credit *to-which* they-*are* accustomed. *This-is what we call a commercial* crisis. *In* extreme cases *there-is* added *a financial* panic *as* groundless *as-the* former *over*-confidence, *and* money *is* borrowed *for short* periods at *a* ruinous rate-*of-interest*. Prices *of* commodities *and* stocks then fall *as-much* below-*the usual* level *as*-they-*had* risen above *that* level *during-the* period *of* inflation. (272)

Exercise 137

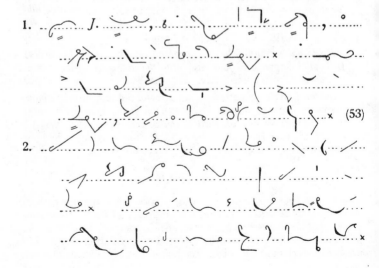

1. (53)

2.

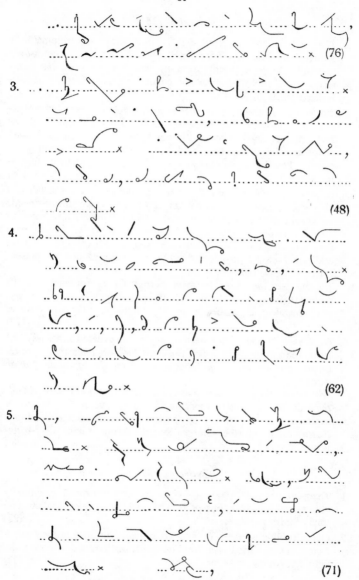

Exercise 138

1. *The* enclosed-bill, received *this*-morning *with your* shipment, *is* returned *because you have* listed *two* items *which-have*-not-*been* received. Will-*you* kindly send-us *your*-bill *for* only *the* items received *and*-another-bill *for-the* remainder *of-the* shipment *when-it-is* dispatched. (47)

2. *Yesterday we*-received *your* cheque *in* settlement *of-your* December-bill. *We*-did-not notice *when-we* forwarded *it to-our*-bank *that-the two* amounts *on-the* cheque did-not agree. One *is for* £39, *and-the* other *is for* £38, *and our*-bank *has* just *called our*-attention *to-the* error. *Your*-bank will-not cash *the* cheque, *of*-course, unless-*the* amounts agree. May-*we* please-*have* another cheque? (76)

3. *Gentlemen, We*-received *this*-morning *your* cheque *for* £300, *and* also *your* post-dated cheque *for* £200. *This*-arrangement *for-the* settlement *of-your*-account *is satisfactory. We-have* also received *your*-order, *but inasmuch-as-the balance* of £200 will-not-*be* paid until *a* month hence, *we-do*-not-*think you-should expect* us *to*-extend additional credit *for*-another £125, *the* amount *of-your* present order, until *the* old debt *is* fully paid.
   We-suggest, *therefore, that-you* permit us *to* forward *a* draft *for-the* £125 *to-the* National-Bank *and* Trust-Company *of-your* city, covering *the* amount *of-this* shipment. *Very*-truly-*yours*, (122)

4. *Gentlemen,* If-*you do*-not need *all-the*-goods ordered now, *why* not let-us send *those* items *which-you* need *for-your immediate*-requirements, *and* forward *your* cheque covering *the* amount *of-those* items?
   We-shall-be very glad *to-give* our *immediate*-attention *to any* part-*of-the* order *that-you* instruct us *to*-send *on-this* basis, *and-we*-hope-*that within a* month or-*two your*-account will-*be in*-such *a* condition *that-we-can* add further-charges covering future orders. *Very*-truly-*yours*, (89)

Exercise 139

1. *There-are* over 2,000,000 motor-trucks *to*day transporting annually about 1,800,000,000 tons *of* freight, including *almost* 200,000,000 tons *of* farm produce. (27)

2. *Over* 20 billion-dollars *is* invested *in public* utilities *in-the* United-States. *Of-this* total *over* 5 billion-dollars *is* invested *in* power *and* light-companies. (27)

3. *Yesterday,* Professor-Jackson, *the distinguished* economist, aroused *a great-*deal-*(of)*-attention by-*his* article *on-the* savings-bank question *which-is-*now receiving so-much-attention *from-the* various political party-leaders. (33)
4. *The* National Bank-*(of)*-Commerce *has* finally completed *its*-arrangements *for* taking *over-the* business *of-the* Hamilton Trust-Company *with-its* total deposits *of more-*than £8,000,000. (30)
5. 7,000 stockholders *of-the General* Construction-Company will share *in-the* dividends just declared by-*the-*directors. *The* dividends *are* $40,000 *to-the* preferred *and* $2,500,000 *to-the* common stock-holders. (39)
6. *The* "Journal-*(of)*-Commerce" *for-the* current-month *publishes an* article *on-the* proposed merger *of-several large* steel *and* iron-companies. (22)
7. *This* article *calls-*attention *to-the* fact *that government-*officials *in-the* Department-*(of)-Trade-(and)*-Commerce *have* approved-*the* merger upon-*the* recommendation *of-the* Board *of* Railway-Commissioners. (31)
8. Professor-Thomas *of-the* Treasury-Department *of-the* Canadian-*Government* states *that-he believes there-*will-*be* no opposition *from* either *of-the* political-parties *to-the* proposed *income-*tax rates. (31)

Exercise 140

1. Belgium *is* one-*(of-the)-most* densely populated countries *in-the* world. *Within an* area *of a* little-*more-*than 11,500 square-miles *is* confined *a* population *of* 9,100,000. *The* mainland *and* adjacent islands *of* Japan cover *an* area *near*ly 183,000 square-miles, *and-have* 92,400,000 inhabitants. *The* British Commonwealth *of* Nations *has a* population *of* 629,000,000 spread *over near*ly 15,000,000 square-miles. (76)
2. *We-*enclose *an* analysis *of-the financial-*position *of-several mortgage and-insurance-*companies *whose* stocks, *we-believe, are* worth *your-*attention. While-*the income from them is-*not *large, we-*feel, *nevertheless, that-the* stocks *are quite* attractive. *You-*will-note-*that in* every case *the* current dividends *are* earned many-times *over, and, inasmuch-as-the* amounts set aside *for* reserves *are becoming larger* each *year, it-is probable that* higher dividends will *shortly be* paid *to-the* stockholders.
We should welcome an opportunity of serving *you, and careful and* prompt-attention will-*be given to any* orders *you-*may *wish to-*place. *Very-*truly-*yours,* (108)

3. *Dear*-Sir, *The* pavement *in-this* street *has-become* broken *in several* places, *thereby* causing considerable *inconvenience to-the people in-this* neighbourhood. Will-*you* kindly *have* someone *from-your*-department *inspect-the* damage, *and-have-the* necessary repairs made? *We*-trust *that-you*-will *give-this*-matter *your* earliest-attention. *Very*-truly-*yours*, (54)